Bible History Made
SIMPLE

Everything You Should
Have Learned
in Sunday School
(and Probably Didn't)

James E. Smith

Copyright © 2009
James E. Smith
All Rights Reserved

Unless otherwise noted, Scripture quotations are taken from THE HOLY BIBLE, NEW INTERNATIONAL VERSION®. NIV®. Copyright © 1973, 1978, 1984, by International Bible Society. Used by permission of Zondervan Publishing House. All rights reserved.

International Standard Book Number: 978-0-89900-992-6

Dedicated To
Dr. Paul and Peggy Johnson
Dedicated Octogenarian Servants
Encouragers
Friends

CONTENTS

Preface		7
1.	The Big Picture	9
2.	Beginnings Period	19
3.	Scattering Period	27
4.	Pilgrim Period	33
5.	Egyptian Period	43
6.	Wilderness Period	51
7.	Conquest Period	61
8.	Judges Period	69
9.	Single Kingdom Period	77
10.	Sister Kingdoms Period	87
11.	Assyrian Period	95
12.	Babylonian Period	103
13.	Persian Period	111
14.	Silent Period	119
15.	Incarnation Period	131
16.	Pouring Period	143
17.	Pauline Period	155
18.	Persecution Period	167
A Final Word		179

NOTE TO TEACHERS OF THIS COURSE

A PowerPoint outline to use in classroom presentation and a file of suggestions by the author for teaching this material is available at www.collegepress.com.

PREFACE

The argument could be made that one's first steps in serious Bible study should be a book-by-book survey of the Bible. That was the path that was laid out for me as a Freshman in the curriculum of Cincinnati Bible Seminary (now Cincinnati Christian University). Certainly there is a place for such surveys. I have felt over the years, however, that even that study should be preceded by one that charts the flow of biblical history. The books of the Bible are not arranged in chronological order. Beginning students are often baffled when jumping back and forth to different historical contexts. This problem is particularly acute in the Major and Minor Prophets.

The purpose of this book is to depict the flow of biblical history from the creation in Genesis to the new creation in Revelation. I have identified seventeen periods of biblical history. The same basic outline has been followed for the Old Testament periods. The sources of information and duration of each period are discussed. A theme Scripture that summarizes the action in the period is suggested. Key players, major events, and great miracles of each period are identified. For each period the special emphasis in God's message is presented. The section called *Christian Application* gives at least one illustration of how events of a given period are used by the New Testament writers to encourage or instruct Christians. Each period concludes with identification of the watershed event that brought the period to an end followed by a summary chart depicting in the most concise way the information concerning the period.

The New Testament periods follow the same outline with minor changes. *Christian Application* becomes *Old Testament Anticipation*. Here I cite some prophetic passage that anticipates the events of the New Testament period.

For the maximum benefit of this book you will need the *New International Version* (NIV) of the Bible. A Bible atlas or good set of maps at the back of your Bible will be helpful.

I am pleased to give credit to the Sunday Evening Bible Fellowship of First Christian Church of Winter Park, Florida, for helping give a title to this book. Of the many fine suggestions I chose to use that of the youngest member of our Fellowship, Miss Veronika Nyberg, who at the time was in the eighth grade at Geneva Christian School.

The title promises to make Bible history simple. I have eliminated citations of Greek or Hebrew words. There is little documentation, except for biblical references. I do not write to impress any reader with my scholarship such as it is. I try in this book to write as I have taught freshman-level classes for forty years.

Simple is a relative term. What is simple for one is painfully difficult for another. I have tried to reduce biblical history to the most basic terms. Beginning students often find biblical names intimidating. For this reason I have supplied a phonetic spelling of names at the first usage. I have adapted, with some modifications, the system employed by the Holman Bible Dictionary.

For dates of kings during the Sister Kingdom, Assyrian, and Babylonian periods I have used the most recent study of Rodger Young, *Journal of the Evangelical Theological Society* 48 (June 2005): 225-248.

Chapter One

The Big Picture

Modern man views history with disdain. Many would agree with Shakespeare that history is "a tale told by an idiot, full of sound and fury, signifying nothing." Others would echo the more blunt assessment of Henry Ford: "History is bunk!" Casual students find history a dull recitation of facts and dates. Believers, however, find God in all history. It is truly HIS-story! The unshakable conviction of the Christian faith is that the Lord rules forever; his throne is from generation to generation (Lamentations 5:19).

A couple of definitions are in order. *History* is that branch of knowledge that records and explains the past. *Bible history* is the recitation and interpretation of the past that is recorded in the Bible.

Nature of the Bible

God-focus. The Creator has seen fit to reveal some of himself, his ways, and his will at various points and in various ways throughout history (Hebrews 1:1-2). This revelation is recorded in the Bible. The Bible, however, not only *contains* the word of God, the Bible in a unique sense *is* the word of God. Christian teaching is that God inspired or guided the biblical writers so that they recorded only what was true and what God intended for mankind to know (2 Timothy 3:16; 2 Peter 1:21). So biblical history is not the history of man or any movement of man; it is God's history. God is the ultimate author. God is the main focus. As every episode unfolds the reader must ask, "Where is God in this? Why does God record this incident? How did God use this incident for his ultimate purpose?"

Christ-focus. The ultimate purpose of God was to bring his Son Jesus into the world to become our Savior. On some level the entire biblical story prior to his birth points forward to his coming. Jesus taught his disciples to look for him in all of the Scripture. *"He said to them, 'This is what I told you while I was still with you: Everything must be fulfilled that is written about me in the Law of Moses, the Prophets and the Psalms.' Then he opened their minds so they could understand the Scriptures"* (Luke 24:44-45).

In the Old Testament Christ is revealed prophetically; in the New Testament he is revealed historically. In the Old Testament Christ appears in shadow, picture, type, and ritual. In the New Testament he appears in substance, person, truth, and reality. The longing of the Old Testament saints for a Redeemer is captured in the words of Job: *"If only I knew where to find him"* (Job 23:3). The satisfaction of New Testament disciples is expressed in these paraphrased words of Philip: *"We have found him!"* (John 1:45).

Without Christ the Old Testament becomes unexplained ceremonies, unachieved purposes, unsatisfied aspirations, and unfulfilled prophecies. The Old Testament can be likened to a mighty river flowing toward the ocean. Remove Christ and there is no place for the river to go. It simply is swallowed up by the sands of time like a river that flows into a desert.

Structure of the Bible

Two main divisions: A casual look at the Bible indicates that it is a collection of sixty-six individual books. These books fall into one of two main divisions called *testaments*. The word testament means *covenant* or *agreement*. The older of the testaments contains the books that were written at least four hundred years before the birth of Christ. These books constitute the Jewish Scriptures to this day. Christians call this division the *Old Testament*. It consists of thirty-nine books. The other books of the Bible were written within sixty years of the death of Christ. These books are called the *New Testament*. Together the two testaments constitute the Christian Scriptures. Christians derive their understanding of God's will and ways from these books.

Variety. The Bible does not display the uniformity that one might find in reading a modern book by a single author. God did not provide the biblical writers with a style manual. Each expressed the message in his own way. So there is great variety within the Bible. One can find in the Bible prose and poetry. There are narratives, census figures, genealogies, letters, songs, sermons, blueprints, laws, visions, parables, and many other types of literature.

Nonchronological. The books of the two testaments are not arranged in the order in which they were written. For example, many scholars think the earliest book of the Old Testament is Job. In the modern Bible, however, Job is book number eighteen. In the New Testament the twentieth book (James) is thought by many to be the first book to have been written. While reading the Bible through from cover to cover is valuable for some purposes, it will not yield an accurate picture of how events actually unfolded.

Similarities. While the two testaments of Scripture are very different, there are also some striking similarities as well. Both testaments begin with a representative man — Adam the son of God (Luke 3:38) and Jesus the Son of God (Mark 1:1). Satan intrudes early in both testaments, first in a garden (Genesis 3), then in a wilderness (Matthew 4). In both testaments God chose to work with a special nation — Israel in the Old Testament (Leviticus 19:2), the church in the New (1 Peter 2:9). A law was given in both testaments. Moses gave Israel a law at Mount Sinai (Exodus 20);

Christ gave a law for his kingdom in the Sermon on the Mount (Matthew 5–7). Both testaments conclude with a prophecy of Christ's coming (Malachi 3:1; Revelation 22:12).

Arrangement of books. The arrangement of Old Testament books resembles that of the New Testament. Both testaments begin with books setting forth *foundational* facts—Genesis-Deuteronomy in the Old, the four Gospels in the New. The foundational books are followed by books setting forth a historical *framework*—Joshua-Esther in the Old; Acts in the New. Next in both testaments comes a section of books *focusing* on everyday problems of believers—Job-Song of Solomon in the Old; Romans-Jude in the New. Both testaments conclude with a section dealing with the *future*—Isaiah-Malachi in the Old; Revelation in the New.

Unity of the Bible

Storyline. In the broadest possible terms one can see the unity of the Bible by comparing the opening chapters of the first book of the Bible (Genesis) with the concluding chapters of the final book (Revelation). The beginning/end comparison is displayed in the following chart.

Harmony of Theme	
In Genesis	**In Revelation**
Creation of Heavens & Earth	Creation of New Heavens & Earth
Beginning of Sin	Destruction of Sin
Beginning of Pain, Sorrow, Suffering, Death	End of Pain, Sorrow, Suffering, Death
Sinful man deprived of Tree of Life—Driven from Paradise	Redeemed Man Eats of Tree of Life—Restored to Paradise
Satan Victorious	Satan Defeated
Man Goes from Life to Death	Man Goes from Death to Life

The Big Picture

The Big Picture

Focus. At the Cross God provided redemption for sinful mankind. This means God paid the required price to release men from the bondage of sin. The required price was the blood of the perfect Lamb of God, Jesus. The New Testament centers redemption in Jesus Christ. He purchased the church with his own blood (Acts 20:28), gave his flesh for the life of the world (John 6:51). As the Good Shepherd, Jesus laid down his life for his sheep (John 10:11). He demonstrated the greatest love by laying down his life for his friends (John 15:13).

Norman Geisler's book *Christ the Key to Interpreting the Bible* (Moody Press, 1975) demonstrated that every section of Scripture, indeed every book of the Bible, points to Christ in some specific way. One could even argue that the Cross of Christ is the focus of the Old Testament, the Gospels, the Book of Acts, New Testament Epistles, and the Book of Revelation as the following diagram illustrates.

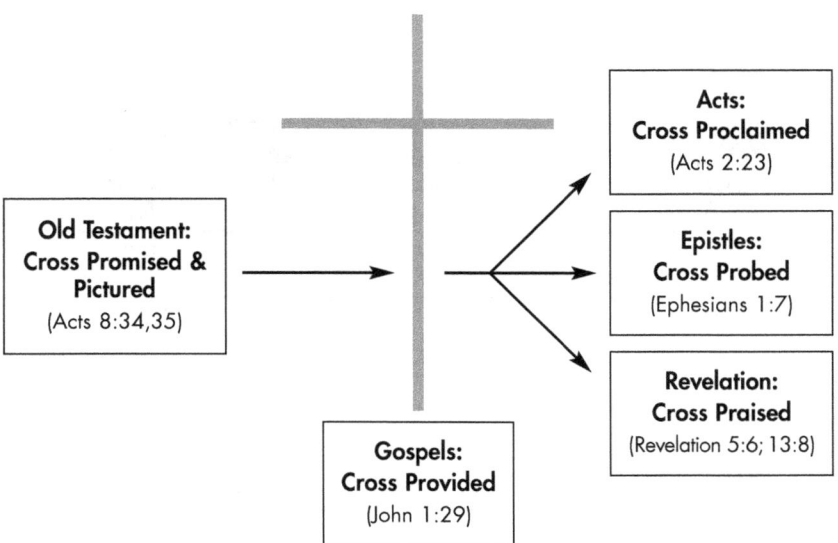

Biblical history is the history of redemption from start to finish. The Patriarchs (fathers of Israel) received the *promise* of redemption. In the rituals of Israel's worship there is a *picture* of redemption. Throughout the history of Israel there is God's *providence* leading to redemption. *Prophecies* of redemption characterize the Old Testament prophets. In the Gospels God made *provision* for redemption by sending his only Son into the world. In Acts there is the *preaching* of redemption. The Epistles stress the *perfection* of redemption. In Revelation the saints *praise* God for redemption.

Biblical Ages

All of the time covered in biblical history falls into three great Ages or Dispensations. An *Age* is a long period of time during which God deals with mankind according to an established set of principles. During each Age men are tested or judged according to their adherence (or lack thereof) to the principles that God has revealed. The three great Ages revealed in the Bible are:

- ❖ **Patriarchal**
- ❖ **Mosaic**
- ❖ **Christian**

THREE AGES OF BIBLE HISTORY		
Patriarchal Age	**Mosaic Age**	**Christian Age**
Time: *Creation to Sinai*	Time: *Sinai to Cross*	Time: *Cross to Coming*
Worship: *An Altar*	Worship: *Tabernacle/Temple*	Worship: *Church*
Sacrifice: *Burnt Offering*	Sacrifice: *Sin/Trespass Offerings*	Sacrifice: *Christ the Lamb*
Leader: *Family Head*	Leader: *Aaron's Family*	Leader: *Christ*
God's Name: *El Shaddai*	God's Name: *Yahweh*	God's Name: *Father*
Illumination: *Starlight*	Illumination: *Moonlight*	Illumination: *Sunlight*
Key Word: *Promise*	Key Word: *Precepts*	Key Word: *Perfection*

The Big Picture

The Big Picture

God's expectations of his people were different in each of these three great ages. Each Age had its own *facts to believe*, *commands to obey*, *warnings to heed*, and *promises to embrace*. What God required and/or permitted in the Patriarchal Age was not necessarily tolerated or required in the Mosaic Age. By the same token, Christians are not required to obey all of the 613 commands in the Law of Moses. The specific terms of salvation after the Cross are not necessarily the same as those prior to the Cross. In the Mosaic and Christian Ages the light of God's truth shone ever brighter. God's nature, will, and goals became ever clearer. The chart above summarizes the major differences between the three great Ages.

Biblical Timeline

Pivotal characters. If one is familiar at all with biblical history, he will have heard of Abraham, Moses, David, and Jesus. Another figure, perhaps not quite as well known, is Nehemiah, the last major character of the Old Testament. Using these five great figures of the Bible as anchors, we can establish a broad outline of biblical history. For now we will use only round figures for dates.

Abraham lived about 2,000 years before Christ. That is easy to remember because we live about 2,000 years after Christ. Roughly 600 years intervened between Abraham and Moses. That puts Moses at roughly 1,400 years before Christ. Between Moses and David roughly 400 years elapsed. That means that David lived roughly 1,000 years before Christ. Roughly 600 years intervened between David and Nehemiah. That puts Nehemiah (end of the Old Testament) at roughly 400 years before Christ. This scheme is easy to remember. It looks like this:

2000 BC Abraham	600	1400 BC Moses	400	1000 BC David	600	400 BC Nehemiah	400	AD 6 Christ

We can remember the five key pegs of the Bible timeline with this mnemonic device:

A Mouse **D**rinks **N**o **C**offee

Timeline books. The timeline for Bible history is established primarily by eleven Old Testament books and five New Testament books. These books may be called *forward motion* books because they move the history of God's people forward in a more or less chronological sequence. They are listed on the top line of the two charts below. Books on the second line may be designated *pause, sidestep* or *focus* books. The material in the focus books must be inserted into the timeline established by the top line.

OLD TESTAMENT TIMELINE								
Genesis	Exodus	Numbers	Joshua	Judges	1&2 Sam	1&2 Kings	Ezra	Nehemiah
⇧Job⇧	⇧Leviticus⇧	⇧Deuteronomy⇧		⇧Ruth⇧		⇧Pss–Hab⇧ 1&2 Chron	⇧Esther⇧ Haggai Zechariah	⇧Malachi⇧

NEW TESTAMENT TIMELINE		
Matthew Mark Luke John	ACTS	
	⇧Romans–2 Thessalonians⇧ Philemon James	⇧1 Timothy–Titus⇧ Hebrews 1 Peter–Revelation

Let's 🛑 right here, catch our breath, and review what we have learned so far. It's as simple as counting to five:

One **Unified Book**
The Bible

Two Great Collections
Old and New Testaments

Three Major Ages
Patriarchal, Mosaic, and Christian

Four Expectations
Facts, Commands, Warnings, Promises

Five Pivotal Characters
Abraham, Moses, David, Nehemiah, Christ

The Big Picture

The Big Picture

Biblical Periods

Bible students generally break up the biblical timeline into periods based on the conditions of God's people, the nature of their leadership, or events that transpired. These periods are marked off on either end by major events designated *watershed events* in this study.

Patriarchal Age. In the Patriarchal Age there were four distinct periods. These periods will be discussed in detail in the chapters that follow. For now just concentrate on mastering the big picture.

1. Beginnings
2. Scattering
3. Pilgrim (2092 BC)
4. Egyptian (1877 BC)

In the Patriarchal Age God was educating his people in some of the fundamental principles of faith and obedience. Try this mnemonic device for recalling the four periods that make up the Patriarchal Age:

Beggars **Sca**re **Pilgrim**s in **Egypt**

The first letter of each word should jog your memory regarding the name of one of the four periods that constitute the Patriarchal Age.

Mosaic Age. More attention is given to the Mosaic Age in Scripture. Ten distinct periods are marked off by watershed events. These ten periods will be discussed in the chapters that follow.

5. Wilderness (1447 BC)
6. Conquest (1407 BC)
7. Judges (1367 BC)
8. Single Kingdom (1043 BC)
9. Sister Kingdoms (931 BC)
10. Assyrian (723 BC)
11. Babylonian (605 BC)
12. Persian 539 BC)
13. Silent (400–6 BC)
14. Incarnation (6 BC)

Jesus lived and died under the Mosaic Age. His death on the Cross as the perfect sacrifice for sin marked the climax of this Age, which lasted almost fifteen hundred years.

Now we have a real challenge. Can you remember the names of the ten periods that make up the Mosaic Age? Try this mnemonic device, or make up your own:

We **C**an **J**oin **Single Sister**s **A**nd **B**ring **P**ickled **S**andwiches **I**n

Christian Age. The first seventy years of the Christian Age are part of New Testament history. These seventy years are divided by watershed events into three periods.

      15 Pouring (AD 30)
      16 Pauline (AD 39)
      17 Persecution (AD 63)

Here is another one of those crazy mnemonic devices to help you remember the good things that God has promised us in the Christian Age. Our Christian promises are just as sweet as:

Plum **P**udding **P**ie

We have completed our bird's eye view of the terrain to be traversed in the following chapters. So then, let's get started.

Chapter Two

BEGINNINGS PERIOD
Downward Spiral of Sin

The source for the first three and a half periods of biblical history is the Book of Genesis, the first book of the Bible. The name *Genesis* means *beginnings*. This is an appropriate name for this first book. Genesis literally describes the beginning of everything—the natural world, sin, marriage, Israel, the hope of salvation through Messiah, just to name a few "beginnings." **Beginnings** is also a very good name for the first period of biblical history.

In scholarly circles the Beginnings Period is called the Antediluvian Period. *Antediluvian* means *before the Flood*, referring to the great worldwide Flood in the days of Noah. The Scripture location for the Beginnings Period is **Genesis 1–8.**

Duration

How much time elapsed before the Flood? That is a difficult question. If one adds together the ages of the ten Beginnings Patriarchs (Genesis 5) at the age when each is said to have fathered his first son, then one would conclude that *at least* 1,656 years elapsed between Creation and the Flood. Christians have never been dogmatic about this time element. Some scholars believe that some names have been omitted from the list in Genesis 5, as is frequently done in biblical genealogies. For the purpose of this crash course in Bible history, we will designate the duration of the Beginnings period as *uncertain*.

Theme Scripture

The first verse of the Bible sets the theme for the Beginnings Period. *"In the beginning God created the heavens and the earth"* (Genesis 1:1). The details of how God created the heavens and earth are part of the report of the Beginnings Period.

Key Players

Seven major characters are in the spotlight during the Beginnings Period.

- ❖ **Adam and Eve**
- ❖ **Cain and Abel**
- ❖ **Seth**
- ❖ **Enoch and Noah**

Adam (*ad´-uhm*) **and Eve** (*eeve*), the only human couple created directly by God's hand, are certainly worthy to be remembered.

Cain (*kayn*) **and Abel** (*ay´-behl*), possibly twin brothers, were the first humans who ever entered the world by the birth process.

Not much is known about **Seth** (*sehth*), except that he became Adam's son through whom the promised Messiah eventually came into the world. For this reason he makes the list of worthies in this period.

Enoch (*ee´-nawkh*) **and Noah** (*noh´-uh*) are the only two men in the Bible who are said to have *walked* with God (Genesis 5:22; 6:9). Both Enoch and Noah also experienced God's salvation. Enoch was saved out of the world so that he never experienced death (Genesis 5:24); Noah was saved through the Flood.

Beginnings Period

Major Events

During the years of the Beginnings Period five major events are recorded, four of which are mentioned in the New Testament writings. Read the New Testament references beside each of the events. Be prepared to share with the class what you learn from the New Testament about these great events of the Beginnings period. Here are the five events:

- **Creation of the world** (Hebrews 11:3; John 1:1-3)
- **A sudden Fall** (2 Corinthians 11:3; 1 Timothy 2:14)
- **A vicious murder** (Hebrews 11:4; 1 John 3:12)
- **A unique rapture** (Hebrews 11:5; Jude 14-15)
- **Corruption of marriage**

Creation (Genesis 1–2). There are two accounts of the creation of the world. In Genesis 1 God created the universe (1:1). He then formed (1:3-13) and filled (1:14-31) the earth in six days. In Genesis 2 God gives us an enlargement or zoom shot of the sixth creative day. We learn that on the sixth day God created man, a garden, special garden animals, and a lovely bride for Adam. That God is the Creator and that man is the special creation of God are foundational truths of the Bible.

Fall (Genesis 3). The term *Fall* refers to the first sin. Adam and his bride Eve chose to disobey the only prohibition God had given them. Eve was deceived by the devil. She in turn led her husband into disobedience. Because of this deliberate sin Adam and Eve were expelled from the garden. They lost access to the tree of life that was in the midst of the garden. The process of death began to work in their lives.

Fratricide (Genesis 4). Life was hard for Adam and Eve outside the garden. Eventually two sons were born. Abel grew up to be a righteous man. He gave to God the best that he had in worship. His brother Cain, however, was evil. He went through the motions of worshiping the Lord, but Cain only gave to God the leftovers of his crops. Cain became jealous because it was obvious that God favored Abel. Eventually Cain **murdered his brother**. God expelled Cain from the area where the human family was rapidly growing. Cain was forced to become a wanderer on the earth. Among Cain's descendants civilization developed. Sin became more prevalent and ugly.

Rapture (Genesis 5:24). Eventually God gave to Eve a son to replace Abel. That son's name was Seth. Among his descendants were some godly people. The godliest of them was Enoch, the seventh from Adam. Enoch walked with God in such intimate fellowship that one day God simply took him to heaven. This is called the **rapture** or translation of Enoch. He was translated or transformed into his immortal heavenly body without passing through death. What happened to Enoch is what will happen to the saints of God who are on the earth at the time Christ returns. Christians will be transformed in a twinkling of an eye into their immortal bodies (1 Corinthians 15:52).

Corruption. In spite of the few bright spots like Enoch, the general tendency of mankind was to become ever more rebellious against God. Marriage as originally established by God broke down. The sons of God—probably the descendants of Seth—married the daughters of men whomever they chose. The reference appears to be to polygamy. About the time of these sinful marriages a group of bullies or tyrants called *Nephilim (ne-fihl-ihm´)* arose on the earth. They filled the earth with violence (Genesis 6:11). The picture is one of complete lawlessness and immorality. Corruption of marriage was the culminating sin of the Beginnings Period.

Great Miracles

Creation was a miracle from start to finish, as was the deliverance of Noah from the Flood. No other miracles are recorded during this period, unless the sign given to Cain was some unspecified miracle (Genesis 4:15 NASB).

Beginnings Period

God's Message

The Bible records the great truths that God revealed over the centuries of human existence. This is called *progressive revelation*. In the Beginnings Period four great truths were revealed.

- **Dignity of man/equality of woman**
- **Structure of marriage**
- **Existence and work of Satan**
- **Need of a Savior**

Human dignity. Human beings were the crown of God's creation. That the creation of man was unique is indicated several ways. Before the creation of man there was deliberation within the Godhead (Genesis 1:26). Only man was made in the image and likeness of God (Genesis 1:26). Only in respect to man is the sexuality—male and female—spelled out. This indicates that sexuality for man is different than for the animal kingdom. The woman was created from a rib taken from the side of man. This signaled that she was not inferior in any way to him. Man and his mate were given dominion over all the other creatures. God spoke directly to the first couple and blessed them. All of these facts indicate the dignity of man and the equality of woman.

Marriage. When God brought the woman to the man, he was inviting the two to form a union (Genesis 2:22). God, in effect, performed the first marriage in the beautiful surroundings of the Garden of Eden. Adam cheerfully and eagerly received his bride. She in no way protested the union. She gladly accepted the name that Adam bestowed upon her (Genesis 2:23). Genesis 2 sets forth the divinely ordained structure of marriage.

From the account in Genesis 2 the following principles about marriage can be deduced. First, marriage is monogamous and heterosexual. God created only one woman for Adam. Second, God sanctioned the union by bringing the woman to the man. True marriage is sanctioned by the governing authority. Third, both the man and the woman freely and eagerly entered into the union. Fourth, the couple was invited to be fruitful and multiply. Sexual union is expected in marriage. Fifth, marriage establishes a bond equivalent to blood kinship. Adam declared: *"This is now bone of my bones and flesh of my flesh"* (Genesis 2:23).

Moses himself (inspired by God) set forth three principles of marriage. *"A man will leave his father and mother and be united to his wife, and they will become one flesh"* (Genesis 2:24).

Satan. The Bible does not say much about how Satan came into being. He simply showed up in the Garden of Eden. Obviously Satan could not have been created in an evil state by God, for that would make God the author of evil. At some point prior to the creation (Genesis 1) one of God's highest angels must have led a rebellion against God (Jude 1:6; 2 Peter 2:4). Satan is not the equal of God; he can only do what God permits him to do. God permitted Satan to tempt Eve in the garden so that she might have the opportunity to make a conscious decision to obey the Lord.

Satan is called *Serpent* in Genesis 3. When he approached Eve he questioned God's goodness and denied God's word. Obviously Satan hates everything that God loves. Satan delights in dragging down people who are made in God's image just as he deceived Eve in the garden.

Savior. The Fall of man into sin demanded countermeasures by the God who loves mankind and wants every person to be saved. Sinful man needed a Savior! God promised that someday One of the descendants of the woman would crush the head of Serpent (Genesis 3:15). This first revelation of the gospel is called by Bible students the *Protevangelium* — the first gospel. This is a way of saying that God would provide victory over Satan and evil. When Christ died on the cross, he dealt a crushing blow to the devil (1 John 3:8).

Christian Application

There are many New Testament references to the early chapters of Genesis. John 1:1-3, for example, makes clear that Christ was present and actively involved in the creation of the world. *"In the beginning was the Word, and the Word was with God, and the Word was God. He was with God in the beginning. Through him all things were made; without him nothing was made that has been made."* (See also Colossians 1:15-16.)

Watershed Event

A watershed event is one that was so important that it closed out one period and introduced a new period of biblical history. The first watershed event was literally a downpour of unparalleled proportions. The Flood is the main concern in four chapters of the Bible. **STOP** right now and read these New Testament references to this great event: Matthew 24:38-39; Hebrews 11:7; 1 Peter 3:20-21; 2 Peter 2:5.

Here are the key facts about the Flood:

- **Extent: worldwide**
- **Sources: rains and fountains of the deep**
- **Duration: over a year**
- **Survivors: eight people + representative animals**
- **Means of survival: a large boat called an ark**
- **Purpose: judgment on sinful mankind**
- **Result: a second start for mankind**

The Flood occurred in the 600th year of Noah's life. Key dates in the rise and fall of the waters are noted. Noah must have been keeping a diary during this world-changing event. The rains fell for forty days and nights, but the waters prevailed over the earth for 150 days. It took seven additional months for the earth to dry out sufficiently for man to again inhabit it. In all, the survivors were on the ark for 370 days.

God found only one righteous man on the earth in the days before the Flood. Noah and his sons (Shem, Ham, and Japheth) and their wives found grace in God's eyes (Genesis 6:8). They demonstrated their obedience to God by building the ark, herding the animals on board, and entering the vessel on the appointed day. The major families of animals were represented by at least one mated pair. Clean animals—those most used by man—numbered either seven or (more likely) seven pairs (Genesis 7:2; see footnote in NIV).

The Flood survivors rode out the Flood on a large vessel called an ark. This vessel was more than one-and-a-half football fields long. It had three decks. The decks were sectioned off for the various animals. The ark was built of gopher wood, which cannot be identified with certainty. The NIV interprets gopher wood to be cypress, which is known to have been used for shipbuilding in ancient times. The vessel was waterproofed with pitch or bitumen. This is a petroleum-based, sticky substance that oozes up from the ground in some areas of the Near East.

The Flood judgment cleansed the world from sin. It enabled mankind to make a fresh start.

Summary Chart

C R E A T I O N	Period # 1 BEGINNINGS PERIOD Genesis 1–8		F L O O D
	Major Players Adam & Eve Cain & Abel Seth Enoch & Noah	**Major Events** Fall A Murder A Rapture Corrupt Marriages	
	Duration At Least 1,656 Yrs.		

Beginnings Period

Chapter Three

SCATTERING PERIOD
Second Chance Wasted

When Noah and his family walked off the ark, they entered a cleansed world. Everything that offended God had been washed away. The ark came to rest in the mountains of Ararat in the region known today as Armenia. From there the Flood survivors gradually migrated southeast down the Tigris-Euphrates river valley. Man was being given a second chance to demonstrate obedience to God.

Because of the major event that transpired, the second period of biblical history may be called the Scattering Period. Scholars refer to this period as the *Postdiluvian* (post-Flood) Period. The Scripture reference for this period is **Genesis 9–11**.

Duration

The Scattering Period started with the exit from the ark. It ended with God's call to Abram. The Scriptures do not state anywhere how long the Scattering Period lasted. Adding up the ages in the genealogy in Genesis 11 indicates that this period lasted *at least* 427 years. Biblical genealogies are "elastic." Generations are frequently omitted. So the actual time between the end of the Flood and the call of Abram cannot be determined. For this reason the duration of both the Beginnings and Scattering periods is *uncertain*.

Theme Scripture

"From one man he [God] made every nation of men, that they should inhabit the whole earth; and he determined the times set for them and the exact places where they should live" (Acts 17:26). The Scattering Period depicts the human race as one family all descended from Noah. Genesis 9–11 describes how this single human family developed into the various nationalities, and by implication, various racial groupings. Yet the emphasis is on the unity of the human race.

Key Players

The major players in the Scattering Period are few: a ship's captain, his three-man crew, and a hunter.

- ❖ **Noah**
- ❖ **Shem, Ham, Japheth**
- ❖ **Nimrod**

Noah is a transitional figure. He should be listed as the first major character of this period. After the Flood, however, the spotlight shifts to Noah's trio of sons, **Shem, Ham, Japheth** (*jay´-fehth*). All present human population has descended from one of those three sons. The final major player in this period is **Nimrod** (*nihm´-rahd*). He is called *"a mighty hunter before the LORD"* (Genesis 10:9). Nimrod was a tyrant, possibly a slave trader, and the first empire builder of history.

Major Events

The information about the Scattering Period is sparse. Four events can be identified.

- ❖ **Noah worshiped**
- ❖ **Man Fell (again)**
- ❖ **People dispersed**
- ❖ **Empire built**

Scattering Period

Worship. The first thing Noah did when he left the ark was to erect an altar—the first altar mentioned in the Bible. Noah wanted to express the gratitude of his family for the deliverance from Flood destruction. Noah's worship consisted of burnt offerings. In a burnt offering the entire carcass of an animal was consumed in the altar fire. Burnt offerings expressed thanksgiving, and symbolized complete dedication to God (Genesis 8:20-21).

Fall. A few years after the Flood Noah fell into sin. He planted a vineyard, grew grapes, made wine, and got drunk. While he was in his tent in a naked stupor, Noah's youngest son Ham entered the tent. Ham then went out and told his brothers. Ham showed disrespect for his father by (1) entering his father's tent, (2) failing to cover his father, and (3) mockingly describing what he saw to his brothers. Shem and Japheth rebuked their brother by their actions. They backed into the tent (so as not to see their father) and covered him (Genesis 9:20-23). The main point is that sin has again entered the picture, destroying the short-lived existence in a sinless world.

Dispersion. Instead of spreading out to fill the earth as God directed, men decided to build a tower and a city—the city of Babylon. Whereas the exact motivations of the builders are disputed, this much is clear. Mankind was defying God's authority. To bring a halt to the building operation God confused the languages of mankind so that the workers no longer could communicate with one another. The people were dispersed. The various language groups began to spread out over the earth as God intended (Genesis 11:1-9).

Empire. Nimrod was a descendant of Ham (Genesis 10:8-12). He is said to have built several cities in southern Mesopotamia (modern Iraq). Then he moved up the Tigris-Euphrates river valley and built another cluster of cities. This may be considered the first empire in history. Nimrod probably built his empire with slave labor. This is another sign of growing sin in the Scattering Period.

Great Miracles

Only one miracle is recorded during the Scattering Period, the confusion of the languages of mankind at the Tower of Babel. Not all of the thousands of modern languages came into being at this time. Probably it was only the great families of language that originated by supernatural act at Babel. During the thousands of years since Babel other languages (like English) developed naturally.

God's Message

Three great revelations took place during the Scattering Period:

- ❖ **Post-Flood precepts**
- ❖ **God's promise**
- ❖ **Noah's prophecy**

Precepts. God gave to Noah some basic precepts to live by after he came off the ark. God specifically authorized man to eat meat (with certain restrictions). He instructed Noah and his family to spread out and fill the earth. Most importantly, God established the foundation of earthly government by authorizing mankind to take the life of those who committed murder (Genesis 9:1-7).

Promise. God entered into a covenant (agreement/promise) with man and animals that he would never again destroy the world by means of a Flood. He indicated that the rainbow would be the sign of that commitment. As long as the earth remains, the rhythm of nature (summer, winter, etc.) will continue (Genesis 9:8-17).

Prophecy. Sometime after the sin of Ham against his father, Noah spoke a prophetic word concerning his sons. He predicted that the descendants of Canaan, the grandson of Ham, would become servants to all the other families descended from Noah. The focus is on the Canaanites because that is the people that later were the near neighbors of the Israelites. Throughout the rest of biblical history the Canaanites were subject first to the Egyptians (descendants of Ham), then to the Israelites (descendants of Shem), and finally to the Persians and Greeks (descendants of Japheth).

Noah also prophesied that someday God would come to dwell in the tents of Shem (Genesis 9:27). This prophecy found its fulfillment when Christ came into the world to live among the Jewish people (Shemites) for about thirty-three years. In the New Testament we read how *"the Word (Christ) became flesh and made his dwelling (lit., tented) among us"* (John 1:14). Noah's prophecy about the coming of God to dwell among the Shemites is the second messianic prophecy (prophecy about Christ) in the Bible. (This prophecy is wrongly interpreted by the NIV, which translates *"may Japheth live in the tents of Shem."*)

Christian Application

Since only three chapters of the Bible are devoted to the Scattering Period we should not expect to find many allusions to this period in the New Testament. This citation from the writings of Peter ties the Scattering Period to the experience of the Christian.

> *God waited patiently in the days of Noah while the ark was being built. In it only a few people, eight in all, were saved through water, and this water symbolizes baptism that now saves you also — not the removal of dirt from the body but the pledge of a good conscience toward God. It saves you by the resurrection of Jesus Christ.* (1 Peter 3:20-21)

Noah and his family passed through the waters of the Flood to inhabit a new world, cleansed from all sin. So the believer passes through the waters of baptism to experience the new world of the Christian life.

Watershed Event

The Scattering Period concluded with God's call to Abram. By biblical data this event can be dated to about **2092 BC**.

Abram was a wealthy merchant who lived in Ur, a major city in southern Mesopotamia (modern Iraq). God told Abram to leave his family and go to a land that he would show him. Abram did not exactly obey what God said. He took his aged father and other family members and migrated up the Euphrates River to a city known as Haran. Initially he did not make it to the Promised Land. In Haran Abram was still in his "comfort zone." The people there spoke the same language, and worshiped the same gods as the people in Ur.

When his father died, Abram received a second call from God to go to a land that God would show him. This time Abram obeyed. He and his wife and servants and nephew journeyed to the land of Canaan.

Summary Chart

F L O O D	Period # 2 **SCATTERING PERIOD** Genesis 9–11		C A L L
	Key Players Noah Noah's Sons Nimrod	**Major Events** Noah's Worship Man's 2nd Fall People Dispersed Empire Built	
	Duration At Least 427 Yrs.		

Scattering Period

Chapter Four

Pilgrim Period
Looking for a City

The Scattering Period saw massive rebellion against God and the dispersion of people under God's judgment. With the third period of biblical history God begins to work with one special people. His plan was to use that special people to bless all other peoples by bringing his Son into this world.

The Pilgrim Period is often referred to as the *Patriarchal* period. A Patriarch is a father or ancestor. In biblical studies the term *Patriarch* is usually restricted to Abraham, Isaac, and Jacob and Jacob's twelve sons.

Open your Bible and read part of Stephen's sermon in Acts 7:2-8. Note how Stephen refers to Abraham as *our father* and sons of Jacob as the *twelve Patriarchs*.

Thirty-five chapters of Genesis are devoted to the Pilgrim Period (**Genesis 12–46**). The number of chapters indicates the importance of this period compared to the two previous periods that we have studied.

33

Duration

The Pilgrim Period begins with God's call to Abram (whose name was later changed to Abraham). That call can be dated to 2092 BC using biblical data.[1] The Pilgrim Period ended about 1877 BC when Jacob and his family migrated to Egypt during a famine. For this event we can coin the term **Eisodus**, which means "the way into" Egypt. This means that the Pilgrim Period lasted **215 years**, or about two centuries.

Theme Scripture

"By faith he [Abraham] made his home in the promised land like a stranger in a foreign country; he lived in tents, as did Isaac and Jacob, who were heirs with him of the same promise" (Hebrews 11:9). This verse highlights the pilgrim nature of the third period of biblical history. The Patriarchs were tent-dwellers. They were looking for a permanent home.

The theme of the Pilgrim Period is *faith tested*. God made wonderful promises to the Patriarchs (Genesis 12:1-3, 7). To all outward appearances it must have seemed to them that those promises were not working out. God promised to make Abraham's descendants as numerous as the stars of the sky; yet for twenty-five years—long past child-bearing age—he had no child by his wife Sarah. God promised that Abraham would be a blessing; yet he seemed to cause trouble for many of those he met along the way. God promised to give Abraham a land; yet that land was already occupied. The same promises were made to Isaac and Jacob. Their faith was also put to the test in similar ways. Yet in spite of outward appearances, the Patriarchs clung to faith in God's word of promise.

---

[1] We arrive at this date by starting with 967 BC for the date of the building of Solomon's temple. We then add 480 years (1 Kings 6:1) to get the date of the Exodus. Add to that 430 years (Exodus 12:40) to get the date when Israel went down into Egypt. Add 130 years (Genesis 47:9) for the date of Jacob's birth. Add 60 years (Genesis 25:26) to get the date of Isaac's birth. Add 100 years (Genesis 21:5) to get the date of Abraham's birth. Subtract 75 years (Genesis 12:4) to get the date of the call of Abraham.

Key Players

The Pilgrim Period takes its name from the three individuals whose journeys in and out of the land of Canaan are full of spiritual lessons for Christians in their pilgrimage through this world. These three pilgrims were:

- ❖ **Abraham**
- ❖ **Isaac**
- ❖ **Jacob**

Pilgrim #1: Abram/**Abraham** (*ayb´-ra-hahm*) was a wealthy merchant whom God called to leave his country and move to a land that he would show him. Here are some basic facts about this great man of faith.

- ❖ **Wife:** Sarai/Sarah (*say´-rye/say´-rah*) (1 Peter 3:6)
- ❖ **Concubine:** Hagar (*hay´-gahr*)
- ❖ **Sons:** Isaac (*i´-zahk*); Ishmael (*ish´-may-el*)
- ❖ **Shining moment:** "Sacrifice" of Isaac (Genesis 22)
- ❖ **Special title:** Friend of God (James 2:23)
- ❖ **Significance:** God's covenant (see later).

Abraham was not a perfect man. At times he doubted God and left the Promised Land. Each time he did, he fell into sin. When he became impatient with God's promise of a son, he tried to "help" God by taking as his concubine (secondary wife) the handmaid of Sarah. He learned the hard way that faith is living without scheming.

Note that Abraham had two I's: Little I = **Ishmael** (by Hagar) and Big I = **Isaac** (by Sarah). Ishmael is the ancestor of the Arab peoples, while the Jews trace their ancestry back to Isaac. Read what Paul in the New Testament said about these two sons (Galatians 4:21-31).

Pilgrim #2: Details about the life of **Isaac,** the promised child, are sketchy. His life is intertwined with that of his father or of his sons in most of the narratives. Here are the important points to remember about Isaac.

- ❖ **Wife:** Rebekah
- ❖ **Twin sons:** Esau and Jacob (Hebrews 12:16)
- ❖ **Shining moment:** Blessing on Jacob (Hebrews 11:20)

Pilgrim #3: For over half of his long life **Jacob** (*jay´-kuhb*) was a swindler, a liar, and a deceiver. Yet God saw in him potential to become a spiritual leader. God revealed himself to Jacob in a dream at Bethel. Though Jacob was totally unworthy at the time, God transferred to him the blessings he had promised to his grandfather Abraham and his father Isaac. Jesus once conversed with a woman at a spot connected with Jacob. Read John 4:5-6. Here are the important facts about Jacob.

- ❖ **Wives:** Leah (*lee´-uh*); Rachel (*ray´-shehl*) — sisters.
- ❖ **Sons:** Twelve — ancestors of the tribes of Israel.
- ❖ **Shining moment:** Led family back to Bethel (Genesis 35)
- ❖ **Special title:** Israel (*ihz´-ray-ehl*)

Major Events

You will recall that a call from God and a great journey of faith marked the beginning of the Pilgrim Period. The lives of Isaac and Jacob were also characterized by journeys, although not so dramatic as that of Abraham. The faith of these men was tested at every campsite. Sometimes their faith was weak. Often they did not live as godly men should live. Frequently they fell into doubt and sin. Aside from the journeys, five other major events transpired during the Pilgrim Period. They are:

- ❖ **A judgment**
- ❖ **A birth**

Pilgrim Period

❖ A test
❖ A marriage
❖ A wrestling match

Judgment (Genesis 19). Because of some family issues, one of Abraham's relatives, Lot, came to reside in the wicked city of Sodom. The city was so immoral that God decided to destroy it. For the sake of Abraham, however, he determined to spare Lot. Angels were sent into Sodom to warn Lot to flee. Lot and two daughters escaped just in time, but Lot's wife looked back to the city as they fled. She was turned into a pillar of salt. God rained down fire and brimstone (sulfur) upon **Sodom and three neighboring cities.** The destruction of these immoral cities was to serve as a warning to other cities throughout the ages. Read what the New Testament says about this great judgment: Luke 17:29; 2 Peter 2:6; Jude 1:7.

Birth (Genesis 21). When Abraham entered the land of Canaan, he was 75. For twenty-five years Sarah was barren. The couple was past the age of childbearing when God informed them that within a year the special child would be born. When Abraham was 100 and Sarah was 90 the child of promise was born. His name was Isaac. Read what the New Testament says about this event in Hebrews 11:11-12.

Test (Genesis 22). Some twenty years or so passed by in silence. God directed Abraham to take his son and offer him as a burnt offering. The pagan religions of that day practiced human sacrifice. This was a test to help Abraham demonstrate his faith and thereby grow in his commitment to God. Abraham and Isaac journeyed to the land of Moriah in the vicinity of what later would be the city of Jerusalem. Isaac questioned his father as they started up the hill about what they would offer as a sacrifice. Abraham replied: *"God himself will provide"* (Genesis 22:8).

Abraham was prepared to carry through on the divine command. At the last minute, a voice from heaven directed Abraham to a sheep caught in a nearby thicket. The sheep was to substitute for Isaac. Abraham had passed the test. Read what the New Testament says about this incident in Hebrews 11:17-19.

Marriage (Genesis 24). As Isaac grew to manhood Abraham became concerned about finding a godly wife for his son. He dispatched a servant with camels loaded with wealth to the city of Haran in northwestern Mesopotamia—the city where Abraham had resided for a time. Some of Abraham's relatives who shared his faith in the Living God still resided there. The servant asked God to guide him in the selection process. The girl that God had chosen for Isaac's bride would be the one who offered to water his camels. The prayer scarcely had been uttered when Rebekah approached the stranger and met the test. The servant told the girl and her family his story. They interpreted what had transpired at the well as a sign that Rebekah should leave with the servant to travel several hundred miles to Canaan to marry a man she had never met. All parties involved in this marriage were exercising great faith. It was important for Isaac, the promised son, to marry only a woman of faith.

Wrestling match (Genesis 32:22-32). For twenty years Jacob resided in Haran with his uncle Laban. There is not much to commend Jacob during these years. He was an unscrupulous and worldly man. Finally God told him to return to the Promised Land.

Returning to Canaan with his family Jacob faced several dangers. One night near the Jabbok River when he was alone, he saw a shadowy figure. He thought this might be Esau or one of his agents. Jacob wrestled with the "man" all night. Toward morning the "man" touched Jacob's hip. Jacob was severely injured. He knew at that moment that he was not wrestling with an ordinary man. At that point Jacob began to pray and beg for a blessing. The shadowy figure turned out to be a manifestation of God. That night God changed Jacob's name to *Israel*, which means something like *he who struggles with God*.

Jacob's night of wrestling with God was a turning point in his life. He did not become a perfect man after that, but he certainly became a more spiritual man. So the story of Jacob is the story of the transformation from scoundrel to saint. After that match beside the Jabbok, Jacob grew into the spiritual head of his family.

Great Miracles

In the Pilgrim Period the conception and birth of Isaac was a miracle (Hebrews 11:11-12). The destruction of Sodom by fire and brimstone from heaven was also a miracle (Genesis 19).

God's Message

Reference already has been made to the great promises that God communicated some nine times to Abraham, Isaac, and Jacob. Scholars refer to this collection of promises as the Abrahamic covenant. In addition to these promises, God granted to Abraham and his descendants five important revelations during the Pilgrim Period:

- ❖ **Melchizedek episode**
- ❖ **Sign of circumcision**
- ❖ **"Sacrifice" of Isaac**
- ❖ **Jacob's ladder vision**
- ❖ **Revelation of God's names**

Melchizedek episode (Genesis 14). After a successful battle with foreign invaders, Abraham encountered the priest-king of Jerusalem. He was not an Israelite, but was clearly devoted to the one true God. Melchizedek (*mehl-khihz´-eh-dehk*) is taken by New Testament writers to be a type or preview of the coming of Christ. Read Hebrews 7:1-10.

Circumcision sign (Genesis 17). When Abraham was 99, God appeared to him and instructed him to circumcise all the males in the household. Thereafter, that rite was to be performed on all males on the eighth day after birth. Circumcision was to be the badge of all those who were part of the special family God chose to work through prior to the coming of Christ.

"Sacrifice" of Isaac *(Genesis 22)*. Abraham's test in the land of Moriah already has been cited as one of the major events of the Pilgrim Period. At that time God made clear the principle of substitution. God did not want human sacrifice. The wages of sin is death. Either the sinner must die, or one must die in his place. No sinful person can die for the sins of another. That is why God permitted an innocent animal to be sacrificed as a substitute for a guilty person. While God does not want or require human sacrifice, he does expect wholehearted commitment and unquestioning obedience from those who worship him. That is the revelation connected with the "sacrifice" of Isaac.

Jacob's ladder *(Genesis 28)*. While fleeing from his brother Esau, Jacob spent a night at Luz (later Bethel). While he slept that night, he had a vision of a ladder stretching from heaven to earth. He saw angels ascending and descending upon that ladder. The ladder symbolized the connecting link between God and man. The angels carried Jacob's prayers heavenward; they also executed God's responses to those petitions. Jesus saw in that ladder a preview of himself (John 1:51). For Christians Jesus is the connecting link to heaven. Through him we pray; through him God answers our prayers.

Name revelations. We sometimes give nicknames to describe something about a person or pet. Names like Slim, Chubby, Moose, and Bubba all convey an image about someone. In the Pilgrim Period God took names for himself or names were attributed to him that convey something about his divine nature. Here are a few of God's names revealed in the Pilgrim Period. *El Shaddai* = God Almighty (Genesis 35:11); *El Elyon* = Most High God (Genesis 14:18); *El Roi* = the God who sees (Genesis 16:13); *Yahweh Yireh* = Yahweh Provides (Genesis 22:14); *Fear of Isaac* (Genesis 31:42); and *Shepherd* (Genesis 48:15).

Christian Application

The New Testament alludes to the Pilgrim Period numerous times. One passage, however, catches the essence of this period and shows how it ties in with the pilgrimage of the Christian. *"For he [Abraham] was looking forward to the city with foundations, whose architect and builder is God"* (Hebrews 11:10).

Abraham traveled about on donkeys or camels. We drive automobiles and fly airplanes. Abraham enjoyed a wonderful walk with the Lord during his lifetime. Yet he knew that something better was ahead for him. So Christians have precious fellowship with God here and now. Like Abraham, however, we look for that city whose maker and builder is God. Two thousand years before Christ spiritual men were searching for the same thing that spiritual men two thousand years after Christ seek.

Watershed Event (Genesis 42–46)

The concluding event of the Pilgrim Period may be called the *Eisodus (ice´-o-dus) — the going into*. About 1877 BC Jacob sent his sons to Egypt because a famine made food supplies scarce in the land of Canaan (*kay´-nan*). Joseph, Jacob's eleventh son, had been sold into slavery by his brothers at the age of seventeen (Genesis 37). Over the next thirteen years Joseph's yo-yo story is a series of promotions and setbacks. Eventually he was made Prime Minister of Egypt. In that position he was able to orchestrate the migration of his family and their favorable location in the land of Goshen. The family of Jacob numbered seventy at this time (Genesis 46:27). This migration to Egypt brought an end to the Pilgrim Period.

Summary Chart

C A L L	Period # 3 PILGRIM PERIOD Genesis 12–46		E I S O D U S
	Key Players	**Major Events**	
	Abraham	A Judgment	
		A Birth	
	Isaac	A Test	
		A Marriage	
	Jacob	A Wrestling Match	
2092 BC	Duration 215 Years		1877 BC

Pilgrim Period

Chapter Five

EGYPTIAN PERIOD
From Slavery to Nationhood

The fourth period of biblical history is called the Egyptian Period because it takes place in Egypt south of Canaan. You can read about the Egyptian Period in the closing chapters of Genesis (**Genesis 47-50**) and the opening chapters of the Book of Exodus (**Exodus 1-15**). Nineteen chapters are devoted to the Egyptian Period.

Duration

The Egyptian Period began with the *Eisodus* in 1877 BC. This is when Jacob's family of seventy souls made its way down into Egypt to escape famine conditions in Canaan. The Egyptian Period ends with the **Exodus** — the going out of Egypt — in 1447 BC. For those interested in knowing how the dates are derived from the biblical data, see note on page 34.

The Scriptures state exactly how long the Egyptian Period lasted. *"Now the length of time the Israelite people lived in Egypt was **430 years**"* (Exodus 12:40).

Scriptural Theme

"I have indeed seen the oppression of my people in Egypt. I have heard their groaning and have come down to set them free. Now come, I

will send you back to Egypt" (Acts 7:34). Deliverance from bondage is the theme of the Egyptian Period. This does not mean, however, that Israel was in bondage for all 430 years of this period. For the first seventy years of this period Joseph was prime minister of Egypt. The Israelites were a favored people. At some point, however, a new dynasty arose that changed the policy regarding the Israelites. The Israelites were subjected to the indignities and rigors of slavery. How long that condition of slavery lasted cannot be determined from Scripture.

Key Players

There are only two major characters in the Egyptian Period — **Joseph** on the front end and **Moses** on the back end of the 430 years.

Joseph (*joh´-sihf*) was sold into slavery in Egypt when he was seventeen. He was thirty when Pharaoh made him Prime Minister of Egypt. Most of the thirteen years intervening were spent in prison. Joseph devised a taxation system that stored up huge supplies of grain during the seven years of plenty. When the famine struck, Joseph let people buy back grain until they ran out of money. Then they had to deed over their private property to Pharaoh, and even sell themselves into slavery to the government, in order to secure grain. So under Joseph's leadership Pharaoh's wealth and power were consolidated. Joseph continued in his position as Prime Minister until his death at age 110.

Moses (*moh´-sihs*) was born about 1527 BC during a time when the Israelites were being persecuted by the Egyptians. He probably would have been slain as an infant were it not for the courage and faith of his parents (Hebrews 11:23). For a time the infant was kept at home. When that became unsafe, his mother engineered a plot to have him "discovered" by Pharaoh's daughter. She fell in love with the baby. Moses' sister Miriam (*mihr´-ih-uhm*), acting as a go-between, arranged to have his mother keep the baby until he was weaned. Then he went to live in the palace with Pharaoh's daughter.

Egyptian Period

For forty years Moses was educated in Egyptian schools (Acts 7:22). According to sources outside the Bible, he was given a command in the military. He is said to have led at least one campaign in Ethiopia. At age forty Moses renounced Egypt (Hebrews 11:24-28). He went out to offer his services to the Israelite slaves. Suspicious of his intentions, the Israelites rejected him. Moses left Egypt to live in the desert (Acts 7:23-29).

For forty years Moses worked for his father-in-law raising sheep. One day he encountered a burning bush. God called to him from the bush. He directed Moses to return to Egypt and lead the children of Israel out of slavery (Exodus 2:11-25).

At age eighty Moses returned to Egypt. He unleashed God's power against Egypt. The Egyptians were forced to release the Israelites.

Moses is mentioned eighty-five times in the New Testament. There is a good summary of his life in Acts 7:27-36 and a wonderful comment about his faith in Hebrews 11:23-29.

Major Events

Three events are highlighted in the Egyptian Period:

- **Preservation of God's people**
- **Persecution of Israel**
- **Plagues against Egypt**

Preservation. As Prime Minister of Egypt, Joseph took steps to preserve his family during a famine. He saw to it that they received adequate food. He settled his family in the region known as Goshen away from the main centers of Egyptian culture. He did not want his people to be unduly influenced by the immorality and idolatry of the Egyptian people.

Persecution. As long as Joseph was alive, the Israelites got along fine in Egypt. Eventually a new line of Pharaohs arose who did not feel any gratitude toward Joseph and his people. As the Israelites continued to increase, the Egyptians felt threatened.

They thought that the Israelites might aid some foreign invader that was intent on overthrowing Egypt. Government policy forced the Israelites to build cities (Exodus 1:11). Still Israel continued to multiply. Finally, the government resorted to population control. All male Israelite children were to be slain at birth.

Plagues. When Pharaoh refused to acknowledge the demands for Israel's release, God unleashed against the Egyptians a devastating series of disasters. These ten disasters are called plagues. The plagues extended over a period of about nine months. See further under *Great Miracles* below.

Great Miracles

Ten plagues manifested God's great power in the land of Egypt. The first two disasters against Egypt were river plagues. The waters of Egypt turned blood red. Frogs came up out of the waters. They covered the land. The third and fourth plagues were nuisance plagues. Lice and flies made life miserable for the Egyptians. The fifth and sixth disasters were related to disease. Egyptian cattle died in large numbers. Boils broke out on the Egyptians. The seventh and eighth disasters affected the possessions of the Egyptians. Hail beat down the crops. Locusts consumed what crops were still standing in the fields. The ninth and tenth plagues are associated with death. Darkness so thick it could be felt came over the land. Finally, God smote the firstborn throughout the land. Now at last the Egyptians were anxious to get rid of the Israelites.

God's Message

Three great revelations occurred during the Egyptian Period:
- ❖ **Death-bed predictions**
- ❖ **Burning bush revelations**
- ❖ **Passover regulations**

Egyptian Period

Death-bed predictions *(Genesis 49)*. The biblical Patriarchs were also prophets. Near the time of their deaths they made predictions about the destinies of their sons. Jacob had something to say about each of his twelve sons. In effect he "demoted" his three oldest sons for deeds they had done over the years. This left the fourth son Judah as the first among the brothers. Jacob foresaw that Judah's descendants would continue in this status of leadership *until Shiloh comes"* (KJV; NASB). (The NIV does not give the best translation at this point.). Many scholars think that *Shiloh* (*Rest Bringer*) is the first proper name given to Christ in the Old Testament. Jesus once said, *"Come unto me, all ye that labor and are heavy laden, and I will give you rest"* (Matthew 11:28 KJV).

Burning bush revelations *(Exodus 3–4)*. At the burning bush God had a conversation with Moses that revealed several things about himself. First, the Lord identified himself as *"the God of Abraham, the God of Isaac, and the God of Jacob"* (Exodus 3:6). Second, God revealed his compassion. He was aware of the misery of his people in Egypt (Exodus 3:7, 9). Third, God revealed his intentions. He planned to bring his people out of bondage and give them a land flowing with milk and honey (Exodus 3:8). Fourth, God revealed his choice. He had chosen Moses to be the agent through whom he would bring about deliverance (Exodus 3:10). Fifth, he revealed his name: *I AM* (Exodus 3:14). God is the Eternal One. His special name *Yahweh* means *he who exists*. English versions generally follow the Jewish custom of substituting the name LORD (all caps) in over 6,500 places where this special name appears in the Old Testament. Sixth, God revealed his power. Moses' staff was turned into a snake, then back into a rod. His hand was made leprous then cleansed (Exodus 4:1-7). Moses is the first person in the Bible whom God empowered to perform miracles as signs that he had been sent from God.

Passover revelation *(Exodus 12)*. Just before the final blow against Egypt (death of the firstborn) Moses was told to establish a memorial feast. Throughout future generations that feast was to be observed by Israelites on the fifteenth day of the first month of the year. Each family was to eat a roasted lamb, with bitter herbs and unleavened bread. These items were to remind the Israelites of how God brought them deliverance from Egyptian bondage. He passed over the houses where he saw the blood of the lamb smeared on the door posts. Salvation came through the blood of the slain lamb.

Paul declared that Christ is the Christian's Passover (1 Corinthians 5:7). He is the Lamb of God that takes away the sin of the world (John 1:29). He makes possible our deliverance from Satan's bondage. It was at a Passover meal in an upper room where Jesus took the cup of juice and the unleavened bread and gave them new meaning for his followers (1 Corinthians 11:23-26).

Christian Application

The New Testament sees spiritual truths illustrated in the crossing of the Red Sea. *"For I do not want you to be ignorant of the fact, brothers, that our forefathers were all under the cloud and that they all passed through the sea. They were all baptized into Moses in the cloud and in the sea"* (1 Corinthians 10:1-4). For Paul baptism was like the crossing of the Red Sea. The Israelites were baptized (immersed) as they left Egypt. Only by crossing through the sea could they have freedom from bondage. So the believer obeys the gospel in baptism. He passes through the waters of baptism to experience a new relationship with the Lord.

Watershed Event (Exodus 14-15)

Some 600,000 Israelite men (Exodus 12:37) left Egypt on the original Passover night. They marched out of Egypt as an organized army, divided into divisions (Exodus 12:41). The Egyptians were so grief stricken that they were glad to see the Israelites finally leave. Scripture makes the point that the Israelites left Egypt on the 430th anniversary of Jacob's entrance into that land (Exodus 12:40).

Egyptian Period

Egyptian Period

The route of Israel's march along the eastern border of Egypt encouraged Pharaoh to think that he could overtake the Israelites and force them to return to Egypt. Pharaoh pursued Israel with six hundred chariots (Exodus 14:13-17). He had the Israelites trapped. The Red Sea was to the east, a mountain range to the south. Pharaoh was pressing in from the northwest. The people saw the danger. They cried out against Moses. Even the great Moses was at a loss to know what to do. The Israelites were trapped.

God told Moses to stretch out his staff over the sea. God made a path for his people through the midst of the waters. A cloud brought darkness to the Egyptians during the night, but light to the Israelites. As they walked across the seabed on dry land, there was a wall of water on both sides (Exodus 14:29).

When the darkness lifted, the Egyptians tried to pursue the Israelites into the sea. When the last Israelite reached the opposite shore safely, the waters came crashing back together. Pharaoh's elite chariot force was wiped out. The victory was celebrated in a song written by Moses. Miriam, Moses' sister, led the women in singing (Exodus 15:1-18).

The Egyptian Period ends with this dramatic **crossing of the Red Sea** about 1447 BC.

Summary Chart

E I S O D U S	Period # 4 EGYPTIAN PERIOD Genesis 47–Exodus 15		E X O D U S
	Key Players Joseph Moses	**Major Events** Preservation Persecution Plagues	
1877 BC	Duration 430 Years		1447 BC

Review Time

1. Can you recall the first four periods of biblical history? Perhaps this partial mnemonic sentence will jog your memory:

   Beggars **Sca**re **Pilgrim**s in **Egypt**

2. In what period would you place . . .
   a. Cain and Abel
   b. Joseph and Moses
   c. Noah and Shem
   d. Nimrod and Japheth
   e. Enoch and Noah

3. What period would you be reading about in . . .
   a. Genesis 3
   b. Exodus 15
   c. Genesis 49
   d. Genesis 15

4. What watershed event came between . . .
   a. Beginnings and Scattering periods
   b. Scattering and Pilgrim periods
   c. Pilgrim and Egyptian periods

Answers (inverted at bottom of page):

1. Beginnings, Scattering, Pilgrim, Egyptian
2. a. Beginnings; b. Egyptian; c. Scattering; d. Scattering; e. Beginnings
3. a. Beginnings; b. Egyptian; c. Egyptian; d. Pilgrim
4. a. Flood; b. Call of Abraham; c. Exodus

Egyptian Period

Chapter Six

WILDERNESS PERIOD
Israel Becomes a Nation

When the Israelites crossed the Red Sea, they were in a wilderness area. A wilderness in the Bible is not necessarily a desert. It is a relatively uninhabited area. The Israelites were in an area called today the Sinai Peninsula. In Moses' day the mountains in the Sinai Peninsula were used by the Egyptians for mining operations. Small tribes in the region migrated from oasis to oasis.

The biblical sources for the Wilderness Period are (1) **Exodus 16–40**, (2) **Leviticus**, (3) **Numbers**, and (4) **Deuteronomy**. Thus a total of 122 chapters (about 13% of the entire Old Testament) discuss or are derived from the Wilderness Period. The amount of biblical text indicates the importance of this period of Bible history.

Duration

The Wilderness Period is one of the shortest periods in the Bible. It began with the crossing of the Red Sea about 1447 BC. It lasted until the crossing of the Jordan River, about 1407 BC. So this period lasted **40 years**.

It took Israel about forty-five days to reach Mount Sinai after departing from Egypt. Moses was in the mountain receiving a law code from God for eighty days. Israel resided in the plain beneath the mountain for another nine months. At that point the Israelites broke camp. They slowly made their way to Kadesh, a southern gateway to Canaan. This journey took eleven months. Then because of their unbelief, God sentenced the nation to wander in the wilderness for another thirty-eight years. Finally in the fortieth year after leaving Egypt Israel emerged from the wilderness to conquer the land east of the Jordan River.

As was the case in the Egyptian Period, most of what we know about the Wilderness Period happened on the front end and back end—within the first two years or the last two years of the forty-year period. The intervening years are virtually a blank.

Scriptural Theme

"He [the Lord] endured their conduct for about forty years in the desert" (Acts 13:18). The phrase ***marching and murmuring*** describes what was taking place in the Wilderness Period. Nowhere in the Bible is the patience of God more obvious. Time and again he put up with complaints, criticism, and outright rebellion on the part of the newly liberated slaves.

Key Players

The superstars in the Wilderness Period are **Moses**, his brother **Aaron** (*awehr´-uhn*), and their sister **Miriam** (*mihr´-ih-uhm*).

Moses. We were introduced to the first eighty years of Moses' life in the Egyptian Period. In the last forty years of his life **Moses** became the most influential figure in Old Testament history. Through Moses God revealed his Law at Mount Sinai. Through Moses God performed miracles for his people throughout their journey. Moses taught the people God's ways. He rebuked them when necessary. He encouraged them when they were depressed. He organized this ragtag bunch of slaves into a nation.

Great as he was, there were failures in Moses' life. He often was discouraged because of the whining of the people and the personal attacks against him. On one occasion God told him to speak to a rock. Instead Moses smote the rock. Out came water. Moses acted as though he had performed the miracle in his own strength. Because of this sin God told Moses he would not be permitted to cross over into the Promised Land of Canaan with his people.

Aaron. Moses' brother **Aaron** failed in his first leadership test. While Moses was in the mountain receiving God's Law, Aaron assisted the people in making an image—a golden calf—to represent the invisible God. In spite of this failing, however, God named Aaron as the first high priest of the nation. More than that, God decreed that all future high priests would have to be direct descendants of Aaron. As high priest Aaron officiated at all the religious holy days. Aaron was at his best when on one occasion a judgment plague was sweeping across the camp. People in the path of the plague were dying right and left. Aaron grabbed his censer—a metal vessel in which incense was burned. He stationed himself in the path of the plague, risking his own life, to offer up the incense of prayer before the Lord for his people (Numbers 16).

Miriam is named as one of the three great leaders of Israel during this period (Micah 6:4). Her leadership seems to have been among the women of Israel. She was at her best when Israel crossed the Red Sea. Miriam led the women in singing on that occasion. She had her bad day when jealousy over the influence of Moses' wife seized her. Miriam persuaded Aaron to join her in challenging the leadership of Moses. God rebuked Miriam by striking her temporarily with the disease of leprosy. Moses prayed for her restoration. Even so, God ordered that Miriam be required to remain outside the camp with other unclean folk for seven days. Thus progress in the march was impeded for a week because of dissension in the ranks of the leadership team (Numbers 12).

Major Events

There are so many major events in the Wilderness Period that it is difficult to know what to leave out. Perhaps the best approach is to categorize them.

Rebellions. On several occasions the Israelites were prepared to stone Moses, appoint a new leader, and return to Egypt. There were, however, three rebellions during this period of particular note. They occurred at Mount Sinai, at Kadesh, and in the Plains of Moab—one might say at the beginning, middle and end of the period.

First, at Mount Sinai, while Moses was receiving the design for the Tabernacle, the people insisted that Aaron make for them a visible god to go before them. With the words of the Ten Commandments ringing in their ears (*Do not make any graven image!*), the people constructed a golden calf. They participated in a drunken orgy as part of the worship of this idol (Exodus 32).

Second, while camped at Kadesh, Korah and Dathan organized a two-pronged attack against the political leadership of Moses and the priestly leadership of Aaron. The rebels were executed by God, some by being smitten by lightning from heaven, the rest in an earthquake (Numbers 16).

Third, in the plains of Moab just before the death of Moses there was another serious rebellion against God. The men of Israel were lured into immoral feasts in honor of the fertility god Baal. The leaders of this rebellion were executed and impaled; a plague smote thousands of the people (Numbers 25).

Battles. Several great battles were fought in the Wilderness Period. Near Mount Sinai the stragglers in the Israelite march were attacked by a desert tribe called the Amalekites. Joshua and the men of war were able to suppress this danger. During the battle they were encouraged by seeing Moses with the staff of God raised high over his head (Exodus 17).

After leaving the wilderness Israel fought two major campaigns against kings who tried to stop their march. Both were easily defeated (Numbers 21).

Just before his death Moses ordered twelve thousand men to fight a holy war against the Midianites who had tried to defeat Israel with magic and with immoral worship. Not one Israelite soldier was lost in battle (Numbers 31).

Wilderness Period

Wilderness Period

Construction. While at Mount Sinai the Israelites undertook a major construction project. They built a portable shrine which they could take with them in their travels. This shrine is called the Tabernacle. The Tabernacle consisted of a tent of two compartments surrounded by a large courtyard. Public worship was conducted only at the Tabernacle (Exodus 25–40).

Censuses. Moses took a census at Mount Sinai to organize the men of Israel into an army (Numbers 1). Another census was taken at the end of the forty years of wandering (Numbers 26). The total military manpower was about the same; but the numbers of some individual tribes were quite different.

Death. The death of Moses must be listed as a major event of the Wilderness Period. Moses was told that it was time for him to die. He climbed Mount Nebo to survey the Promised Land from afar. Then he died. An interesting thing happened after his death (Deuteronomy 34) which you can read about in Jude 1:9.

Great Miracles

The Wilderness Period was characterized by miracles, literally on a daily basis. Every day God provided **manna**—a special food—from heaven. This provision continued until the Israelites were in the Promised Land where the crops were abundant. Twice God brought forth **water from a rock**. Twice God brought **quail** into the camp in large numbers so that the people could have meat. When people were bitten by poisonous snakes, a **symbol of a snake** was erected in the camp. When stricken people looked to the elevated serpent in faith they were healed. Jesus once used this incident to teach about his crucifixion (John 3:14).

God's Message

A great deal of revelation took place during the Wilderness Period. We can isolate four areas that qualify as the most important.

- ❖ God's Law
- ❖ Worship system
- ❖ Balaam's prophecies
- ❖ Moses' predictions

God's Law. The Jewish rabbis count 613 commands in the Law of Moses, 365 negative, the rest positive. These commands include criminal law, worship law, civil law, and special law — laws designed to set Israel apart from all other nations. God's Law established a judicial system, made provisions for a future king, and set apart one tribe (Levi) and one family within that tribe (Aaron's) to manage religious affairs. Much of the Law of Moses mirrors the laws of other nations of that time. Some of it, however, is revolutionary. The insistence on one God and no idols was unique, as were the high sexual standards taught by the Law. God's Law is summarized in the Ten Commandments (Exodus 20). Displayed below is a paraphrase of the Ten Commandments.

TEN COMMANDMENTS SUMMARIZED Exodus 20:1–17	
Duty toward God	Duty toward Man
1. No other gods. 2. No images. 3. No misuse of God's name. 4. Remember Sabbath.	5. Honor parents. 6. No murder. 7. No adultery. 8. No stealing. 9. No lying. 10. No coveting.

Worship system. God revealed to his people how, when, and where they were to approach him. Worship under the Sinai covenant centered in the Tabernacle. It was administered by a priesthood from the family of Aaron led by the high priest. People gathered in the courtyard to present one or more of five basic offerings. These five offerings are easily remembered with the acronym **BuMP SiT**. The consonants stand for **B**urnt Offering, **M**eal Offering, **P**eace (fellowship) Offering, **S**in Offering, and

Wilderness Period

Wilderness Period

Trespass Offering. It is beyond the scope of this crash course to describe these offerings any further. Suffice it to say that each offering had a distinctive purpose; each pointed forward to the perfect sacrifice of Christ in some specific way.

There was no prescribed congregational worship under Moses' Law. The Sabbath was a day of rest and reflection at home with one's family. Three times a year the men were required and the women were permitted to attend national feasts to remember great events in the history of Israel. The annual festivals can be remembered with the acronym **PUF WATT**. These letters stand for: *P*assover, Unleavened Bread, First Fruits, *W*eeks, Atonement, Trumpets, *T*abernacles. Those italicized were mandatory. Again, the details of these feasts are beyond the scope of this study. Suffice it to say, that each of these feasts pointed forward to the coming of Christ in some very unique way.

The Book of Hebrews in the New Testament is full of teaching pointing out the rich spiritual significance of the Tabernacle and its worship system.

Balaam's prophecy. Balaam (*bay´-luhm*) was a Gentile who had a reputation for accurate predictions and magic spells. He was hired by the king of Moab to put the whammy on Israel so that the Moabites could defeat them in battle. God told Balaam that he should not use his gifts to try to curse a people that God had blessed. Balaam really wanted to go. So God allowed him to go to teach him (and us) a lesson (Numbers 22).

When he reached the region of Moab, Balaam was taken to a hill overlooking the camp of Israel. Balaam thought he could bribe God with sacrifices to get permission to curse Israel. He was wrong. Every time Balaam opened his mouth, out came a blessing rather than a curse. Four times Balaam spoke, each time saying very positive things (Numbers 23-25). God was speaking through his mouth as surely as he had spoken through the mouth of his donkey en route to Moab.

In Balaam's fourth message God revealed something that was to happen in the distant future. A *star and a scepter*—a great

Ruler—was to arise in Israel. This Ruler was to crush all the enemies of God's people (Numbers 24:17-19). Many scholars think that Balaam, under inspiration from God, was speaking about Christ.

Take time to read how the New Testament uses Balaam as a representative of false teachers in the Christian Age (2 Peter 2:15; Jude 1:11; Revelation 2:14).

Moses' predictions. As a prophet Moses was in a class by himself (Deuteronomy 34:10). In one of his last discourses Moses predicted that when Israel was settled in the Promised Land the people would become unfaithful to God. They would be carried away into captivity in a distant land. When they repented, they would be restored to their homeland (Deuteronomy 28-30). The books of Ezra and Nehemiah record the fulfillment of Moses' predictions.

Moses also reports something God had revealed to him. Someday God would raise up for Israel a *prophet like Moses*. All people would be expected to listen to him (Deuteronomy 18:14-19). The *prophet like Moses* was Christ (Acts 3:22f; 7:37).

Christian Application

Several New Testament passages have already been cited that refer to the events of the Wilderness Period. Here is another example from the pen of Paul that alludes to several of the events of the Wilderness Period. Can you identify them?

> *They were all baptized into Moses in the cloud and in the sea. They all ate the same spiritual food and drank the same spiritual drink; for they drank from the spiritual rock that accompanied them, and that rock was Christ. Nevertheless, God was not pleased with most of them; their bodies were scattered over the desert. Now these things occurred as examples to keep us from setting our hearts on evil things as they did. Do not be idolaters, as some of them were; as it is written: "The people sat down to eat and drink and got up to indulge in pagan revelry." We should not commit*

Wilderness Period

Wilderness Period

sexual immorality, as some of them did – and in one day twenty-three thousand of them died. We should not test the Lord, as some of them did – and were killed by snakes. And do not grumble, as some of them did – and were killed by the destroying angel. These things happened to them as examples and were written down as warnings for us, on whom the fulfillment of the ages has come (1 Corinthians 10:2-10).

Watershed Event (Joshua 1–3)

For a time Israel camped on the eastern side of the Jordan River at a place called Shittim in the Plains of Moab. Just across the river was the fortress of Jericho, the first objective of the Israelite army once the invasion of the Promised Land began. Thirty days after the death of Moses (Deuteronomy 34:8) God gave the orders for the Israelites to cross the river into Canaan. This **crossing of the Jordan River** in 1407 BC marked the end of the forty-year Wilderness Period.

Summary Chart

CROSSING a Sea	Biblical Period # 5 WILDERNESS PERIOD Exodus 15–Deuteronomy 34		CROSSING a River
	Major Players Moses Aaron Miriam	**Major Events** Rebellions Battles Censuses Construction Death	
1447 BC	Duration 40 Years		1407 BC

59

Review Time

1. Can you name the first five periods of biblical history?
2. Can you tell the duration of each of the periods?
3. In which period would you place the following clusters?
   a. Moses, Miriam, Aaron
   b. Shem, Ham, Japheth
   c. Adam, Eve, Seth
   d. Abraham, Isaac, Jacob
   e. Joseph, Moses
4. Indicate what period you would be in if you were reading the following chapters of the Bible:
   a. Genesis 5
   b. Numbers 21
   c. Deuteronomy 31
   d. Exodus 5
   e. Leviticus 16
   f. Genesis 49
   g. Genesis 15

---

1. Beginnings, Scattering, Pilgrim, Egyptian, Wilderness.
2. Beginnings, Scattering = uncertain; Pilgrim = 215 yrs; Egyptian = 430 yrs.; Wilderness = 40 yrs.
3. a. Wilderness; b. Scattering; c. Beginnings; d. Pilgrim; e. Egyptian.
4. a. Beginnings; b. Wilderness; c. Wilderness; d. Egyptian; e. Wilderness; f. Egyptian; g. Pilgrim.

Wilderness Period

Chapter Seven

CONQUEST PERIOD
Claiming an Inheritance

The descendants of Abraham, Isaac, and Jacob lived with the promise of a land inheritance through the Pilgrim Period (215 yrs.), the Egyptian Period (430 yrs.), and the Wilderness Period (40 yrs.). Now it was time to claim the inheritance.

God did not hand over the land of Canaan to the Israelites on a silver platter. They had to fight for the right to possess that land. The Scripture source for the Conquest Period is the **Book of Joshua** and seven chapters in the **Book of Judges** (chs 1–2; 17–21), a total of 28 chapters. For the first time in our study we encounter the problem that not all the history in the Bible is arranged in chronological order.

Duration

The Conquest Period began when the Israelites crossed the Jordan River about 1407 BC. This period of biblical history has three distinct phases. The first seven years, under the leadership of Joshua, were *terrific* years. The Israelites, fighting together as a nation, smashed through all opposition that the Canaanites threw in their paths. The next thirteen years were *tribal* years, when the individual tribes fought to clear out pockets of Canaanite resistance in their respective areas. Some tribes were successful, some failed, and some never even tried. The last twenty years of the Conquest Period were *terrible* years for Israel. Idolatry came out of the closet, sanctioned by no less a figure than the grandson of Moses (Judges 18:30).[2] Immorality and violence were rampant. A civil war nearly wiped out one of the tribes.

The Conquest Period ended with the first of several foreign invasions of Canaan in 1367 BC. So the Conquest Period, like the preceding Wilderness Period, lasted **forty years**.

Scriptural Theme

"He [the Lord] overthrew seven nations in Canaan and gave their land to his people as their inheritance" (Acts 13:19). This verse captures the theme of the Conquest Period—invasion and inheritance. The seven nations in Canaan included Hittites, Girgashites, Amorites, Canaanites, Perizzites, Hivites, and Jebusites (Deuteronomy 7:1). After conquering these peoples, the land of Canaan was divided up among the twelve tribes of Israel.

Key Players

There are really only three major characters in the Conquest Period:

- ❖ **The chief:** Joshua
- ❖ **The old man:** Caleb
- ❖ **The prostitute:** Rahab

Chief. Because of their faith that God would give Israel the land, Joshua and Caleb alone out of 600,000 fighting men counted in the census at Sinai were permitted to enter the Promised Land. Joshua (*jahsh´-ew-uh*) succeeded Moses as the leader of the nation. Under his capable leadership Israel smashed the resistance of the corrupt Canaanites.

---

[2] The *King James Version* and *New American Standard Bible* make the renegade priest a grandson of Manasseh rather than Moses. The *New International Version* has the correct reading.

Conquest Period

Old man. Caleb (*kay´-luhb*) was a leader in the tribe of Judah. At eighty-five years of age he was still willing to take on the giants who lived in the area that was assigned to him (Joshua 14:1-15).

Prostitute. Rahab (*ray´-hab*) makes the list of most important characters because she was the only Canaanite to throw herself on the mercy of the Lord. As a result this harlot found salvation for herself and her family when Jericho was captured. See what the New Testament says about Rahab in Hebrews 11:31; James 2:25.

Some other figures deserve secondary listing among the key players of the Conquest Period.

Achan is prominent in a negative way. He violated the rules at Jericho and stole some of the spoils of the city. Because there were stolen goods in the camp of Israel, God did not aid the Israelites in their next battle. Achan and his family accomplices were exposed by God and executed (Joshua 7).

Grandsons of Aaron and Moses figure prominently in the Conquest Period. **Phinehas**, grandson of Aaron, was intensely loyal to the Lord. When he heard of two of the tribes building an unauthorized altar, he was ready to go to war. An investigation indicated that the altar was really a monument, not a worship altar. Civil War was averted because these tribal brothers sat down and talked through their differences (Joshua 22).

The spiritual opposite of Phinehas was **Jonathan**, Moses' grandson. He hired out to a man named Micah to become his priest at a private idolatrous shrine. Later Jonathan set up idolatrous worship in the city of Dan in northern Canaan (Judges 17–18).

Major Events

For the Conquest Period we will group the major events under headings that spell the word **BACK**. After 470 years away from Canaan, the Israelites were BACK in the land of their ancestors Abraham, Isaac, and Jacob. The major events of the Conquest Period are:

- ❖ Battles
- ❖ Allotments
- ❖ Commitments
- ❖ Konfusion (confusion)

Battles. As the name of this period suggests, the forty years of the Conquest Period involved almost continual fighting. Under Joshua's leadership there were three main military successes, one setback. Jericho (*jeh´-rih-koh*) was the first victory. After seven days of merely marching around the city, the walls supernaturally crumbled. This fortress fell to the Israelites with very little effort on their part (Joshua 6). See how the New Testament explains the collapse of Jericho's walls (Hebrews 11:30). Overconfident because of the Jericho success, the Israelites attacked Ai (*ay´-i*) without adequate forces, without prayer, and without God's help. They were defeated (Joshua 7:3-5).

The Ai defeat was quickly reversed when Joshua got back in tune with the Lord. The first great military test came when a number of kings in southern Canaan banded together to resist Israel. Joshua launched a surprise attack against the Southern Coalition and defeated them. God assisted the effort by answering a prayer of Joshua and causing the sun to stand still in the midst of the sky (Joshua 10).

An even stronger coalition of Canaanite kings formed in the northern part of Canaan. For the first time the Israelites went up against an army that had chariot units. Again Joshua won a smashing victory (Joshua 11).

Allotments. After the united tribes of Israel had broken the back of the Canaanite resistance, the land of Canaan was divided and allocated to the various tribes. The tribal boundaries are carefully mapped out in the Book of Joshua. Tribal areas were assigned by lot, a process equivalent to "drawing straws" (Joshua 14–20).

Joshua charged the individual tribes of Israel to "clean out" the pockets of resistance in their tribal territories. Following the path of compromise, some tribes failed to carry out God's orders to drive out the Canaanites (Judges 1:22-36). One tribe was even forced to relocate some of its clans because they could not or would not defeat the local Canaanites (Joshua 19:47; Judges 18).

Commitments. Three times during the Conquest Period Joshua called upon the tribes to recommit themselves to the Lord. At Gilgal, the first camping spot in Canaan, Joshua ordered all males who had not been circumcised during the forty years in the wilderness to undergo this important covenant ceremony. At the same time Israel celebrated a Passover feast, the first recorded celebration since leaving Mount Sinai.

Joshua led the Israelites to the Shechem area in order to renew their commitment to the Lord. Half of the tribes assembled in front of Mount Ebal (*ee´-buhl*), half in front of Mount Gerizim (*geh´-rih-zihm*). The blessings and curses stated in God's Law were read. After each pronouncement the people on one or the other of the mountains shouted a hearty *Amen*. This ceremony of recommitment to God was planned by Moses before his death (Joshua 8:30-35).

Toward the end of his life Joshua called the people back to Shechem (*sheh´-khuhm*). He gave them his farewell message. In it he urged the Israelites to put away their foreign gods. He challenged them to choose that very day to serve the Lord. At that time Joshua spoke those famous words: *"As for me and my household, we will serve the LORD"* (Joshua 24:15).

Konfusion. I am spelling *confusion* with a K to emphasize just how confused the times were. The last six chapters of Judges belong chronologically to the period immediately after the death of Joshua. These chapters tell two ugly tales, one of idolatry, the other of immorality. The murderous rape of a Levite's concubine led to a devastating civil war. All the tribes were united against the tribe of Benjamin (*behn´-juh-mihn*) because the elders refused to surrender the rapists/murderers for justice. Thousands of men on both sides were slain. By the end of the conflict only 600 men of Benjamin remained (Judges 19–21).

Great Miracles

Aside from the miraculous crossing of the Jordan River that inaugurated the Conquest Period, only two miracles are recorded during this period. First, the walls of Jericho came crashing down without being battered by the Israelites. Second, at some point during the Battle of Beth-horon (*behth-hoh´-rahn*) Joshua prayed for the **sun to stand still**. The Lord fought for Israel by hurling down great hailstones against the enemy.

God's Message

God spoke on numerous occasions during the Conquest Period. Two revelations, however, stand out. One was at the beginning of the Conquest Period, the other toward its end. These were:

- ❖ **Captain of the Lord's host**
- ❖ **Angel of the Lord**

Captain. Just before the battle at Jericho Joshua encountered an armed warrior who identified himself as the Captain of the Lord's host. This was not a man or an angel; he was a manifestation of God himself. Theologians call such appearances by God *theophanies.* In this case God appeared in battle garb to let Joshua know that he would be leading his people in the upcoming fight to take control of Canaan. The Captain revealed to Joshua the divine plan for capturing the city of Jericho (Joshua 5:12–6:5).

Angel. The second great revelation of the Conquest Period is recorded in Judges 2:1-5. The Angel of the Lord appeared to rebuke the Israelites for having failed to carry through the total judgment upon the Canaanites. Since they had not been willing to carry out God's orders, the messenger announced that God would leave the Canaanites to become "thorns" in the sides of the Israelites. Some think this angel/messenger (the Hebrew word can mean either) was a prophetlike figure. Others think he is a theophany (manifestation of God) like the Captain of the Lord's host.

Christian Application

"For if Joshua had given them rest, God would not have spoken later about another day. There remains, then, a Sabbath-rest for the people of God" (Hebrews 4:8-9). God swore that the generation of Moses would not enter into his rest, symbolized by the land of Canaan (Psalms 95:11). Joshua did lead the next generation into Canaan; but that did not totally fulfill God's promise of rest. There yet remains for Christians a rest such as Joshua was incapable of ever giving. Jesus, however, leads his people into that rest—God's heavenly rest.

Watershed Event (Judges 3:8)

The Conquest Period ended when the Israelite conquerors were themselves conquered by a foreign invader about **1367 BC**. The invader was named **Cushan**. He had a nickname: *Rishathaim* = Double Wicked. He came from an area in northwest Mesopotamia. Cushan was probably a Hittite. For eight years the Israelites were victims of oppression by this invader.

Summary Chart

C R O S S Jordan	Biblical Period # 6 CONQUEST PERIOD Joshua + Judges chs		C U S H A N Invades
	Key Players Joshua Caleb Rahab	**Major Events** Battles Allotments Commitment Konfusion	
1407 BC	Duration 40 Years		1367 BC

Chapter Eight

JUDGES PERIOD
Israel's Dark Ages

Israel drifted away from the Lord after the death of Joshua. In order to shake up and wake up the Israelites, God brought foreign invaders into Canaan. Israel was oppressed by ruthless foes. In their suffering the Israelites repeatedly cried out to the Lord for deliverance. God responded by raising up a series of deliverers called Judges to defeat the oppressors.

The history of the Judges Period is found in **Judges 3–16**, the **Book of Ruth** and **1 Samuel 1–7**. Twenty-five chapters of Scripture describe events in the Judges Period.

Duration

The Judges Period began with **the invasion of Cushan** "the double wicked" about 1367 BC. Fourteen Judges were raised up by God to bring deliverance to Israel. Twelve of these are mentioned in the Book of Judges, and two more in 1 Samuel. The last of the Judges was Samuel. Toward the end of his judgeship the elders of Israel demanded that Samuel anoint for them a permanent leader—a king like all the other nations. The anointing of Israel's first king took place about 1043 BC. So the Judges Period lasted **325 years**.

Scriptural Theme

"After this, God gave them judges until the time of Samuel the prophet" (Acts 13:20). The biblical Judges did not wear black robes and wield gavels. A biblical Judge was a Spirit-filled leader raised up by God to deal with a specific crisis in Israel. Some of the Judges, like Eli, also occupied another office. Eli was Israel's high priest. Samuel the prophet was the last of these Judges.

Key Players

Of the fourteen Judges mentioned in the Bible, four are of particular interest:

- ❖ **A Prophetess:** Deborah
- ❖ **A General:** Gideon
- ❖ **A Strongman:** Samson
- ❖ **A Man of Prayer:** Samuel

Prophetess. Deborah (*dehb´-aw-rah*) was a wife and mother. She is the only female Judge. She was accustomed to settling disputes among Israelites while sitting under a certain palm tree that came to be known as the Palm of Deborah. This woman was also a prophetess. That means that she received direct revelation from the Lord. During her days Israel was being oppressed by a resurgent Canaanite kingdom led by Jabin (*jay´-bihn*), probably a descendant of the Jabin in the Conquest Period. Jabin's general was named Sisera (*sihs´-uhr-uh*). He had nine hundred iron chariots with which he invaded Israel from time to time to demand tribute money for Jabin.

Deborah encouraged Barak (*bay´-rak*) to raise an army and fight the invader. Barak refused to accept the assignment unless Deborah accompanied him to the battle. This she did. In the midst of a blinding rainstorm the Israelite troops charged down Mount Tabor and caught the heavy chariots in mud in which they could not maneuver effectively.

Sisera fled from the battle scene on foot. He took refuge in the tent of a Kenite woman named Jael (*jay´-uhl*). He thought he would be safe. While he was sleeping, however, Jael drove a tent peg through his temple. Thus because of the leadership of Deborah and the courage of Jael Israel was delivered from the terrible oppression of Sisera.

The story of Deborah, Barak, Sisera, and Jael is told in Judges 4, and retold in poetic form in Judges 5.

General: **Gideon** (*gih´-dih-uhn*) was hiding his stash of grain in a winepress to keep it from being seized by the Midianites during their annual incursion into the land. The angel of the Lord appeared to Gideon. He commissioned Gideon to deliver Israel from the Midianites.

Gideon raised an army of several thousands. The Lord told Gideon that his army was too large. Victory with a large army over an enemy would only give glory to man, not God. Gideon put his troops through two tests that reduced their number to three hundred. Each man was given a jar, a torch, and a trumpet. Concealing their torches with their jars, the three hundred positioned themselves around the Midianite camp. In the dead of night Gideon gave the order. The jars were smashed, the torches held high, and the trumpets were blown. The Midianites tumbled out of their tents.

Hearing the trumpets and seeing the lights on the surrounding hills the Midianites thought they were being attack by an army of thousands. In the darkness some of the Midianites fought each other; the rest fled. Gideon sent messengers to summon the rest of the army. Then he pursued the Midianites across the Jordan River. Gideon eventually caught up with the Midianites and crushed them (Judges 6–8).

Strongman: **Samson** (*sam´-suhn*) was reared as a Nazirite from birth. This meant that he was never to drink wine or cut his hair or touch anything that was dead. When Samson grew to manhood, he became a ladies' man. More than one Philistine woman played him for a fool. His troubles with these women triggered a twenty-year campaign of personal revenge against the Philistines (*fih-lihs´-teens*), who were the oppressors of Israel in his days. For example, Samson went to a Philistine city and waylaid thirty men in the dark, confiscating their clothing. Single-handedly Samson burned the fields and vineyards of the Philistines. On another occasion the strongman slew a thousand Philistines with the jawbone of a donkey.

A woman—presumably a Philistine—finally nagged Samson into telling her the secret of his strength. Delilah then lulled Samson to sleep and cut off his hair. His strength immediately left him. The Philistines put out Samson's eyes and placed him in irons (Judges 16:1-22). Samson's story ends on a triumphant note as he pulled down the pillars of the Philistine temple, killing more of the enemy in his death than he had killed in his life (Judges 16:23-30).

Samson was full of faults. Yet God used him for two decades to keep the Philistine menace in check.

Man of prayer: **Samuel** (*sa´-mew-ehl*) like Samson was dedicated to the Lord from birth. In fact, Samuel was raised by the priest Eli at the Tabernacle. While still a boy, God called Samuel to be a prophet (1 Samuel 3). As he grew up, he had the reputation of never being wrong in his predictions (1 Samuel 3:19-21). Like Samson he fought the Philistines. Unlike Samson, the man of prayer was able to achieve a lasting victory over them. The Philistines did not enter Israel again during the life of Samuel (1 Samuel 7:13).

Major Events

Five major events took place during the Judges Period. These are:

- ❖ **Victory over Sisera**
- ❖ **Victory over Midian**
- ❖ **Exploits of Samson**
- ❖ **Call of Samuel**
- ❖ **Capture of the ark**

Judges Period

The first four of these events we already have described under the Key Players section. The **capture of the ark** took place during Samuel's boyhood. The Israelites lost a battle to the Philistines. The Israelites thought that they had lost because they did not have the ark of God with them on the battlefield, so they sent for the ark. The next day the Israelites were again defeated. The ark was captured. News of the defeat and capture of the ark reached Eli, the thirteenth Judge of Israel. The old man was so distraught that he fell off a stool and broke his neck.

The Philistines took the ark as a trophy to the temple of their god Dagon (*day´-gahn*) in Ashdod (*ash´-dahd*). The capture of the ark of God by the Philistines was certainly one of the worst disasters to ever strike Israel in its long history. Yet through this incident God taught the idolatrous Philistines that he was superior to Dagon (1 Samuel 4–5).

Great Miracles

The Judges Period was full of heroic actions and great military victories, but few miracles. In fact, Gideon made this comment: *"Where are all his wonders that our fathers told us about?"* (Judges 6:13). Apparently Gideon had never seen a miracle until the time that an angel of God appeared to him. The angel told Gideon to place an offering of meat and bread on a rock. The angel touched the offering with the tip of his staff. Fire sprang up from the rock and consumed the offering. At the same moment the angel disappeared (Judges 6:21). Gideon requested another miracle just before he engaged the Midianites in battle. He put out a lamb's fleece overnight. He asked first that the fleece be wet with dew the next morning, and the ground around it dry. So it happened. The following day he asked for this miracle to be reversed (Judges 6:36-40).

An angel directed Samson's parents to put an offering on a rock. A flame went up from the rock toward heaven. The angel ascended in the flame (Judges 13:20). Probably Samson's feats of strength can also be classified as miracles.

When the ark of God was captured by the Philistines, God demonstrated his powers in several ways. During two nights the statue of Dagon fell over on its face before the ark. God smote the Philistines with a plague of tumors (1 Samuel 5:1-4, 12). Contrary to their animal instinct two cows pulled a wagon carrying the ark of God to the land of Israel without trying to turn back to their bawling calves (1 Samuel 6:10-14). God smote a number of Israelites who showed lack of respect by looking into the ark (1 Samuel 6:19).

God's Message

In the days of the Judges *"the word of the Lord was rare; there were not many visions"* (1 Samuel 3:1). Most of the revelations from God came toward the end of the long period of the Judges. The exceptions were visits by the angel of the Lord (a manifestation of God himself) to Gideon (Judges 6) and Samson's parents (Judges 13). Three other revelations are worthy of note:

- ❖ **Prediction of a future king**
- ❖ **Prediction of removal of Eli's house**
- ❖ **Revelations to Samuel**

Future king. Hannah (*han´-nuh*) was the mother of Samuel. At the time Hannah brought her son to the Tabernacle, God inspired this woman to sing a prophetic song. The last lines of that song speak about worldwide judgment and a king who would be exalted (1 Samuel 2:10). Many scholars think that Hannah is referring to Christ. If so, then Hannah is the first woman to utter a messianic prophecy — a prophecy that announces the coming of Messiah or Christ.

Faithful priest. Eli's sons were corrupt priests. Eli, the high priest, should have removed them from office. Eli, however, does not seem to have been a disciplinarian. An anonymous man of

Judges Period

God (prophet) appeared to rebuke Eli. The prophet announced that Eli's two sons would both be killed on the same day. Eventually Eli's father's house—the family of Aaron—would be removed from office. God would raise up a faithful priest. In that day the priestly house would serve under the supervision of this anointed one (1 Samuel 2:27-36). Many scholars think that the faithful priest is Christ. Christians are the priestly house that serves God under his supervision.

Samuel revelations. While he was still a child, Samuel received revelations from God. The exact nature of these revelations is not made clear. *"The LORD was with Samuel as he grew up, and he let none of his words fall to the ground. And all Israel from Dan to Beersheba recognized that Samuel was attested as a prophet of the LORD"* (1 Samuel 3:19-20).

Christian Application

> *I do not have time to tell about Gideon, Barak, Samson, Jephthah, David, Samuel and the prophets, who through faith conquered kingdoms, administered justice, and gained what was promised; who shut the mouths of lions, quenched the fury of the flames, and escaped the edge of the sword; whose weakness was turned to strength; and who became powerful in battle and routed foreign armies* (Hebrews 11:32-34).

In these verses Christians are being challenged to endure great hardship and attempt great feats through faith of men like the Judges.

Watershed Event (1 Samuel 8–10)

Samuel was a great leader, but not a good father. His sons were corrupt. Yet Samuel appointed them to assist him in governing the land. He may have intended that they succeed him when he died. About **1043** BC the elders of Israel came to Samuel and asked him to anoint a king for them. They did not want Samuel's sons stepping into their father's sandals. They wanted a permanent succession of rulers like all the surrounding nations.

Samuel was deeply hurt. He prayed about the request. God authorized him to anoint Israel's first king. God brought Saul the son of Kish to Samuel's home. Samuel privately anointed him as king. Shortly thereafter at a public gathering God pointed to Saul as his choice for king. Saul was anointed with oil. With the resignation of Samuel and the anointing of Saul the Judges Period came to an end.

Summary Chart

C U S H A N Invades	Biblical Period # 7 JUDGES PERIOD Judges–Ruth + Samuel chs		C H O O S E King
	Key Players Deborah Gideon Samson Samuel	**Major Events** Sisera Victory Midian Victory Samson Exploits Samuel's Call Ark Captured	
1367 BC	Duration 325 Years		1043 BC

Judges Period

Chapter Nine

SINGLE KINGDOM PERIOD
National Greatness

Israel's monarchy got off to a rough start. Saul had lukewarm support for his reign, until he was able to prove himself. In time, however, Saul demonstrated that he was a good military leader. Saul, however, lacked the obedient spirit that God required in the man who ruled his people. He eventually lost the support of Samuel. At that point Saul no longer had access to divine guidance for his reign.

Single Kingdom or United Monarchy is the designation for that period in which all the tribes of Israel were serving one king. The history of the Single Kingdom Period is found in **1 Samuel 8–1 Kings 11**. In addition, this material is amplified in **1 Chronicles** and **2 Chronicles 1–9**. This adds up to 97 chapters of the Bible. Not since the Wilderness Period have so many chapters been devoted to a biblical period. In addition most of the biblical books of Psalms, Proverbs, Ecclesiastes, Song of Solomon, and possibly Job were written during this period. The amount of text derived from this period and/or describing this period indicates that the Single Kingdom Period is one of the most important of the biblical periods.

Duration

The Single Kingdom Period began with the anointing of King Saul about 1043 BC. The Old Testament does not indicate how long Saul reigned, because some of the numbers have fallen out of the text in 1 Samuel 13:1. Paul says in Acts 13:21 that Saul reigned forty years; but Paul may be including the years that Saul's son ruled a portion of the country after his father's death. David ruled just over forty years. Solomon likewise ruled forty years. The Single Kingdom Period came to an end shortly after the death of Solomon when ten tribes refused to recognize Solomon's son as king. This occurred about 931 BC. So the Single Kingdom Period lasted roughly 1043–931 BC, or about **112 years**.

Scriptural Theme

"He [Solomon] sent the people to their homes, joyful and glad in heart for the good things the LORD *had done for David and Solomon and for his people Israel"* (2 Chronicles 7:10). This verse portrays the Single Kingdom Period as a time of great material blessing. From a loose confederation of tribes Israel had became a prominent nation. David expanded the borders of the nation to the limits stipulated in God's original promise (Genesis 15:18). Revenue poured into Solomon's kingdom from land and sea trade. Rulers from distant lands came to marvel at the wealth and wisdom of Solomon.

Key Players

A host of interesting characters in supporting cast roles parade across the stage of history during the Single Kingdom Period. Among them are princes and princesses, priests, prophets, and generals. Without question, however, the superstars during the Single Kingdom Period were the three kings who ruled Israel:

- ❖ **Saul**
- ❖ **David**
- ❖ **Solomon**

Single Kingdom Period

Single Kingdom Period

King Saul. Not a great deal is known about the three plus decades of Saul's reign. God chose Saul to become the first king of Israel in order to fulfill the request of Israel's elders to give them a king like all the nations. At the start of his reign Saul was humble and devout. While many mocked him as unworthy of kingship, Saul quickly demonstrated that he was good at military tactics. He capably defended the borders of Israel from surrounding enemies, especially the Philistines with whom he was constantly in a state of war. Saul seems to have been possessed by a demonic spirit that from time to time drove him to fits of rage. The first king was wounded in battle with the Philistines in 1010 BC. He fell on his own sword rather than permit himself to be taken alive by the enemy.

King David. When God rejected Saul because of disobedience, Samuel the prophet was dispatched to Bethlehem privately to anoint the boy David as future king. As a boy David was summoned to the court of Saul to provide music for the ailing king. He briefly became one of the king's armor-bearers. In his late teens David catapulted into the national spotlight when he single-handedly slew the giant Goliath. During this period David was given a military command. He rose quickly through the ranks. He became the best of friends with the king's son Jonathan and married the king's daughter Michal.

Fearing for his life, eventually David was forced to flee from the court of Saul. For about three years he was a fugitive living in the wilderness of Judea. His life was in constant danger. Saul's death led to a civil war among the tribes over who would be king. At age thirty David finally won the support of all the tribes.

As king of Israel, David concentrated on expanding the borders of his kingdom. He also was inspired by God's Spirit to pen at least seventy-five of the poems in the Book of Psalms.

King Solomon. As a teenager Solomon inherited a secure kingdom. His forty-year reign was noted for peace and prosperity. Solomon was considered the wisest man of his day. He was a prolific writer. Some of his writings—Proverbs, Ecclesiastes,

Song — are found in our Bibles. Solomon was also famous for his building accomplishments, the most notable of which was the Jerusalem temple.

Major Events

Seven major events transpired during the Single Kingdom Period:

- ❖ Saul's Disobedience
- ❖ Goliath's Defeat
- ❖ David's Danger
- ❖ David's Anointing
- ❖ David's Adultery
- ❖ David's Flight
- ❖ Solomon's Temple

Saul's disobedience (1 Samuel 13, 15). On two occasions Saul disobeyed the direct instructions given to him from God through the prophet Samuel. During the Philistine war Saul failed to wait for Samuel to come to offer sacrifices for the troops at Gilgal (1 Samuel 13). The second occasion was when Saul failed to execute all the Amalekites as ordered by Samuel (1 Samuel 15). After the first act of disobedience Samuel announced that Saul's dynasty would not survive, i.e., his son would not follow him on the throne. After the second disobedient act Samuel announced that God had rejected Saul personally. From this time forward God withdrew his influence and direction in Saul's reign.

Goliath's defeat (1 Samuel 17). A Philistine giant named Goliath (*guh-li´-uhth*) intimidated the armies of Israel for forty days. While taking supplies to his brothers in the battle zone, the youth David (he was about nineteen) saw the intimidation. He volunteered to face Goliath on behalf of Saul's army. Reluctantly the king allowed the shepherd to go into combat. Using his sling David brought down the giant. He then cut off his head. Saul's men were so charged by what they saw David do that they won a smashing victory over the Philistines that day. The incident is important because it catapulted David into the national spotlight.

David's danger (1 Samuel 18–22). As David's popularity grew among the soldiers and people, Saul became jealous to the extreme. He came to view David as a threat to his throne. Saul used various schemes to bring about the death or downfall of David. It became Saul's obsession to kill the perceived rival. David was forced to flee into the wilderness for his safety. Saul pursued him in the wilderness intermittently for several years. There were narrow escapes for David; but each time God delivered him from his foe. Finally, the pressure became too great for David. He fled to the country of the Philistines for refuge.

David's anointing (2 Samuel 2, 5). After Saul's death the tribe of Judah recognized David as king almost immediately. The other tribes were suspicious of David, since he had spent the previous seven months working with the Philistines. David ruled Judah for 7 ½ years. During that time the other tribes rallied around the surviving son of King Saul. There were skirmishes between the two sides. When Saul's last son was assassinated by his own men, the tribes quickly recognized David as their king. So David was anointed three times—once privately by Samuel while he still a boy, once by the tribe of Judah, and finally by all of the Israelite tribes.

David's adultery (2 Samuel 11). During his reign David secured the frontiers of Israel on all sides. He was a great king, and greatly beloved by his people. His biggest shortcoming was when he committed adultery with Bathsheba, the wife of one of his captains. Then to cover up her pregnancy, David had this captain placed on the front lines in battle so he would be killed. David then married Bathsheba. This private sin was exposed and rebuked by the prophet Nathan. The prophet warned that from that day forward David's reign would experience difficulties. And so it happened. Within David's family a son raped his half-sister then was killed by her brother. Eventually a large number in Israel turned against David.

David's flight (2 Samuel 15–18). Absalom, David's son, killed his half-brother then fled to escape any possible punishment by David. Eventually he was permitted to return to Jerusalem. Then Absalom began slowly to undermine his father's reign. Eventually he had enough support to launch a full-scale rebellion against his father. David was forced to flee from Jerusalem to safety across the Jordan River. Absalom's army pursued David. A battle was fought in which Absalom was defeated. Absalom himself was found hanging by his hair from a tree. Joab, David's general, slew him, against the orders of his king.

Solomon's temple (1 Kings 6–8). When Solomon became king, his first priority was to build a glorious temple for the Lord in Jerusalem. With the help of his friend King Hiram of Tyre, Solomon built what surely must have been one of the wonders of the ancient world. The temple was roughly modeled after the tabernacle that had been built during the days of Moses, except it was much larger. It has been estimated that to reproduce Solomon's temple today would cost in excess of a billion dollars. Ironically, under the Old Testament worship system no one ever was allowed to see the interior of the temple except the priests who ministered there.

Great Miracles

Miracles were not common during the Single Kingdom Period. Two events are worthy of note. Both came in response to prayers. A plague was stopped by the prayer of David before it struck Jerusalem (2 Samuel 24:16). When Solomon had finished praying at the dedication of the temple, fire came down from heaven and consumed the burnt offering on the altar (2 Chronicles 7:1).

God's Message

A tremendous amount of revelation was given by God during the Single Kingdom Period. God inspired David and others to pen most of the psalms found in our Bibles. God also inspired Solomon to pen Proverbs, Ecclesiastes, and Song of Solomon. This simple introduction to Bible history is not the proper place to discuss these entire books of Scripture. There are, however, other revelations that are imbedded in the historical material. Three of these revelations are the most important.

- ❖ **Anointing revelations**
- ❖ **Covenant with David**
- ❖ **Temple revelation**

Anointing revelations. God revealed to Samuel that Saul was coming to Ramah seeking his father's lost donkeys. God instructed Samuel to anoint Saul privately as the first king of the nation *(1 Samuel 9)*. When Saul proved unworthy of the crown, God commissioned Samuel to go to Bethlehem to anoint his successor. As the sons of Jesse paraded before him, God revealed to Samuel that young David was the choice to be the next king *(1 Samuel 16)*. So the Lord actually selected Israel's first two kings. The prophet Samuel anointed both of them.

Covenant with David *(2 Samuel 7)*. David desired to build a house for his God. God, however, revealed to Nathan that David was not to build the temple. That job was to be undertaken by David's son. Although David would not build a house for God, the Lord promised to build a house (dynasty) for David. As long as there was a throne, David's descendants would sit upon that throne. The throne of David's kingdom would last forever. The occupant of that throne would be a son of God in a very special sense. Today Jesus sits on David's throne, which is really God's throne (1 Chronicles 29:23). He rules eternally over his kingdom, thus fulfilling the prophecy of Nathan.

Temple revelation (1 Kings 8). When Solomon completed the temple in Jerusalem, the priests carefully installed the Ark of the Covenant into the holiest part of the temple. As the priests withdrew from the Holy Place a cloud filled the temple. The priests could not perform their service because of the cloud, for the glory of the Lord filled the place (1 Kings 8:11). This glorious cloud indicated that God had made Solomon's temple his earthly abode.

Christian Application

Jesus once referenced the Single Kingdom Period in order to illustrate to his audience the great privilege that was theirs to have him in their midst. *"The Queen of the South will rise at the judgment with the men of this generation and condemn them; for she came from the ends of the earth to listen to Solomon's wisdom, and now one greater than Solomon is here"* (Luke 11:31). Jesus was referring to the visit of the queen of Sheba described in 1 Kings 10.

Watershed Event (1 Kings 12)

After Solomon died, his son Rehoboam was readily accepted as king by the tribe of Judah. The northern tribes, however, demanded that Rehoboam come north to negotiate with them before they gave him recognition. They were tired of the high taxes under Solomon, and the apparent favoritism that he showed Judah and Jerusalem. Rehoboam went to Shechem to meet with the tribal elders. He refused, however, to yield to any of their demands. The northern elders stormed out of the meeting. They proclaimed one of their own, Jeroboam (sorry about the two kings having soundalike names), as their king. The anointing of Jeroboam and consequent division of the nation marked the end of the Single Kingdom Period. The division of the kingdom occurred about 931 BC.

Single Kingdom Period

Summary Chart

C H O O S E King	Biblical Period # 8 **SINGLE KINGDOM PERIOD** 1 Samuel 8–1 Kings 11 + 1 Chr + 2 Chr chs		S P L I T Kingdom
	Key Players Saul David Solomon	**Major Events** Saul Disobeys Goliath's Defeat David's Danger David's Anointing David's Adultery David's Flight Solomon's Temple	
1043 BC	**Duration** **112 Years**		931 BC

Review on next page

85

Review Time

1. Name the four periods of the Patriarchal Age.
2. Name the first four periods of the Mosaic Age.
3. Place the following clusters in the proper period:
   a. Gideon, Deborah, Samson
   b. Saul, David, Solomon
   c. Moses, Joseph
   d. Abraham, Isaac, Jacob
   e. Noah, Nimrod, Shem
   f. Joshua, Caleb, Rahab
   g. Moses, Miriam, Aaron
4. Which period(s) lasted . . .
   a. 215 years?
   b. 430 years?
   c. 40 years?
   d. 112 years?
   e. 325 years?

---

1. Beginnings, Scattering, Pilgrim, Egyptian.
2. Wilderness, Conquest, Judges, Single Kingdom.
3. a. Judges; b. Single Kingdom; c. Egyptian; d. Pilgrim; e. Scattering; f. Conquest; g. Wilderness.
4. a. Pilgrim; b. Egyptian; c. Wilderness, Conquest; d. Single Kingdom; e. Judges.

Single Kingdom Period

Chapter Ten

SISTER KINGDOMS PERIOD
Quarreling Sisters

Following the death of Solomon the great kingdom forged through the military efforts of Saul and David split into two sister kingdoms—Israel in the north, Judah in the south. These kingdoms spent the next two centuries (for the most part) quarreling. This is a difficult period for Bible students because there are two sets of kings. The Scripture material is sometimes hard to follow. The writer treats Israel's history for a number of years. Then he goes back, picks up the history of Judah and advances it to a point beyond where he left off with Israel. Then he goes back and picks up the history of Israel where last he left off and moves it forward beyond were he left off with Judah. This may be compared to the way a person walks, advancing first the one foot, then the other. So we might say that the biblical history walks us through the Sister Kingdoms Period.

The history of the Sister Kingdoms or Divided Monarchy Period is recorded in **1 Kings 12–2 Kings 17**. This material is amplified in **2 Chronicles 10–29**. So 48 chapters are devoted to the Divided Monarchy.

Duration

The split in the Kingdom of David/Solomon took place about 931 BC. The Sister Kingdoms Period ended when the city of Samaria, capital of the Northern Kingdom, was captured by the Assyrians in 723 BC. Many of the citizens of the northern tribes were relocated to distant parts of the Assyrian Empire. Those who remained in the territories of the former kingdom gradually intermarried with Gentiles and emerged as the Samaritans of the New Testament period. So the Sister Kingdoms Period lasted about **208 years**.

Scriptural Theme

"When all Israel saw that the king refused to listen to them, they answered the king: 'What share do we have in David, what part in Jesse's son? To your tents, O Israel! Look after your own house, O David!' So the Israelites went home" (1 Kings 12:16). The northern tribes—called Israel or Ephraim—ceased to render allegiance to the house of David. Thus the unified kingdom, ruled by David and Solomon for seventy-three years splintered into two tiny kingdoms.

Key Players

During the course of its history the Northern Kingdom (Israel) had nineteen kings from nine different dynasties or families. During the same time frame the Southern Kingdom (Judah) had eleven rulers. During the two centuries of the Sister Kingdoms Period ten individuals played key roles. These can be broken down into categories to facilitate memorization.

Three northern kings: **Jeroboam** (*jeh-roh-boh´-am*) was the first northern king. He founded a national religion to rival the Jerusalem temple. **Ahab** (*ay´-hab*) was the seventh king in the north. He permitted the practice of the Baal religion alongside the official calf religion. **Jehu** (*jey´-hew*) was the tenth northern king. He launched an all-out assault on the Baal religion. Jehu was ruthless in the elimination of the influence of Jezebel.

Two wicked queens. **Jezebel** (*jehz´-eh-bell*): A foreign princess and devout worshiper of the god Baal who married Ahab. She

Sister Kingdom Period

brought an army of false prophets with her with the intent of making Baal worship the official religion of the Northern Kingdom. She launched a persecution against the prophets of the Lord. Ruthless and cunning, Jezebel let no one stand in her way. After Ahab's death Jezebel continued to wield influence through her two sons who followed Ahab on the throne. Her daughter also became ruler of the Southern Kingdom.

Athaliah (*ath-uh-lih´-ah*): the daughter of Jezebel. We might call her Jezebel, Jr. She was even more ruthless than her mother. When her son the king was killed, Athaliah seized the throne of Judah by murdering all the male members of the royal family. Were it not for the fact that one infant-descendant of David was preserved in the temple, the line of David would have been totally extinguished. After seven years of terror, Athaliah was killed. The rightful king was then installed on the throne.

Two Northern prophets: God's response to the influence of Jezebel and the incursion of the Baal cult into Israel was to raise up the E-team. **Elijah** (*e-li´-jah*) was a powerful prophet raised up in the midst of a persecution of God's prophets. He challenged the Baal prophets to a showdown on Mount Carmel. Elijah was famous for numerous miracles. He was the founder of prophetic schools. Elijah left this world in a chariot of fire and whirlwind (2 Kings 2). **Elisha** (*e-li´-shuh*) was Elijah's assistant and successor. He performed miracles equal to those of his mentor.

Three Southern kings: Each of the three was a reformer for at least part of his reign. Scripture regards them, on balance, as good kings. **Asa** (*a´-suh*) was the third southern king. He cleaned the idols out of Jerusalem, even the idol of his own grandmother. Asa won a smashing victory over an Ethiopian army. Asa's faith grew weaker in old age. He was diseased in his feet, yet failed to call upon the Lord (1 Kings 15).

Jehoshaphat (*jih-hahsh´-uh-fat*) was the fourth southern king. He continued the reforms of his father Asa. Jehoshaphat's basic mistake was to enter into alliances with the corrupt kings of the

Northern Kingdom. On the plus side he enacted educational and judicial reforms in Judah. Twice Jehoshaphat nearly died in war while assisting Northern kings. Jehoshaphat's biggest mistake was taking Jezebel's daughter for the wife of his son.

Joash (*joh´-ash*) came to the throne as a boy. He was guided in his youth by an old priest. Joash bypassed the religious establishment to go to the people for funds to make temple repairs. He put a "Joash" collection box in the temple. After his mentor died, Joash became hard. He refused to listen to God's prophets. One prophet (the son of his former mentor) was killed in the temple on orders from the king. Joash gave temple vessels to a foreign invader to avoid an attack. He was assassinated by some of his officials (2 Kings 11–12).

Major Events

Five events had significant impact during the Sister Kingdoms Period:

- ❖ **Calf religion founded**
- ❖ **Carmel showdown**
- ❖ **Jehu revolution**
- ❖ **Revivals in the south**
- ❖ **Attack against David's house**

Rival religion (1 Kings 12). Jeroboam I, the first king in the North, thought he could not allow his subjects to travel to Jerusalem for festivals at the temple. He decided to establish a rival religious system. Temples were built at two locations in order to make the new cult more convenient. The priesthood was opened up to any who wished to train for it. The king appointed himself high priest. Golden calves were fashioned. Originally the calves were not considered representations of God; they probably were portrayed as the sacred animals on which the invisible God rode. (Most gods of that day were thought to ride on the back of a sacred beast.). As time went on, however, the golden calves were worshiped as idols. This counterfeit religion continued to thrive in the north until the day that kingdom ceased to exist. Over time, however, more and more pagan practices were incorporated into this cult.

Carmel showdown *(1 Kings 18)*. During the reign of Ahab and Jezebel, Elijah challenged the prophets of Baal to a showdown on Mount Carmel. Four hundred of the Baal prophets showed up, along with multitudes of people and the king. Elijah proposed that the prophets of Baal build an altar, prepare a sacrifice to Baal, the weather god, and then pray for him to send the rains. The Baal prophets jumped at this opportunity. They conducted their rituals around the altar for hours, prodded by the sarcasm of Elijah. The Baal prophets chanted, bounded on to the altar, whirled about, and cut themselves with knives all to no avail. By three in the afternoon they were exhausted.

Elijah built a simple altar of twelve stones (representing the twelve tribes) and prepared his sacrifice. He had the sacrifice and altar drenched with water multiple times. Then he prayed a simple prayer. God answered by fire, consumed the sacrifice and even the water about it. The multitudes then publicly committed themselves to the Lord. Elijah ordered them to execute the Baal prophets in compliance with the stipulations of God's Law concerning false prophets. Elijah then went to the summit of Carmel and prayed earnestly for rain. In short order the rains came again to the land.

Jehu revolution *(2 Kings 9–11)*. The campaign against Jezebel and her pagan ways reached a climax when a prophet of God anointed Jehu, an army general, as king. Jehu rode back to the capital from the outpost where he was stationed. The army was in full support of his bid for the throne. The king of Judah, who was the nephew of the king of Israel, happened to be visiting. When the two kings rode out together to meet the general, Jehu slew them both. Then he proceeded to the palace where he ordered Jezebel flung from her window. Jehu vented his hatred for the woman by driving his chariot back and forth across her dead body. Jehu went on to engineer the execution of seventy other relatives of Ahab, forty-two princes of Judah who were coming to give aid against Jehu, and all the worshipers of Baal. Although Jehu was zealous for the Lord, he went about his work in the wrong manner. The end does not justify the means. This revolution in the north took place in the year 841 BC.

Revivals in the south *(2 Chronicles 14)*. As noted earlier, both Asa and Jehoshaphat led reform movements in the south. This involved removal of pagan idols, cleansing of the temple, and renewal of the commitment of the people to the Lord.

Attack against the house of David *(2 Chronicles 28)*. This must be an important event because it is noted not only in Kings and Chronicles, but also in the Book of Isaiah. Ahaz *(ay'-haz)* was king of Judah at the time. He was not a good king, but he was the legitimate representative of the house of David. Two neighboring kings (Syria and Israel) banded together to attack Ahaz. This was not an invasion for spoils or kingdom expansion; it aimed to remove Ahaz from the throne and replace him with a king who would cooperate with the regional kingdoms in withstanding Assyria, a new threat in the area. God protected Ahaz, not because he deserved it, but because of the promises God had made much earlier to David. The invasion fizzled. It was at the time of this invasion that one of the greatest of the prophecies about Christ was uttered. Read it in Isaiah 7:14.

Great Miracles

After the days of Moses, miracles were not conspicuous in the history of Israel. That changed in the Sister Kingdoms Period. For a period of about forty years there was an outpouring of divine power through the prophets Elijah and Elisha. Here is a partial list of their miracles:

Food multiplications (1 Kings 17:15f; 2 Kings 4:1-7, 42-44)
Resurrection (1 Kings 17:19-21; 2 Kings 4)

Sister Kingdom Period

Fire from heaven (1 Kings 18:38; 2 Kings 1)
"Rapture" of Elijah (2 Kings 2)
River parted (2 Kings 2)
Water purified (2 Kings 2:21f)
Food purified (2 Kings 4:38-40)
Bodily healing (2 Kings 5)
Floating ax head (2 Kings 6:1-6)
Bodily harm inflicted (2 Kings 5:26-27; 6:18-23)

God's Message

As in the previous period, again there was an outburst of divine revelation during the Sister Kingdoms Period. At least nine prophets are named in the historical records. In addition there were several anonymous prophets. Six great prophets who wrote entire books of the Bible were also active during this period. These were:

- **Obadiah (*oh-buh-di´-uh*):** *Prophet of Edom's Doom*
- **Joel (*joh´-ehl*):** *Prophet of Pentecost*
- **Jonah (*joh´-nuh*):** *Prejudiced Prophet*
- **Amos (*ay´-mahs*):** *Prophet of the Plumb Line*
- **Hosea (*hoh-say´-uh*):** *Prophet of God's Compassion*
- **Isaiah (*i-zay´-uh*):** *Gospel Prophet*

Christian Application

Jesus mentioned events of the Sister Kingdoms Period to expose Jewish prejudice.

> "I tell you the truth," he continued, "no prophet is accepted in his hometown. I assure you that there were many widows in Israel in Elijah's time, when the sky was shut for three and a half years and there was a severe famine throughout the land. Yet Elijah was not sent to any of

them, but to a widow in Zarephath in the region of Sidon. And there were many in Israel with leprosy in the time of Elisha the prophet, yet not one of them was cleansed – only Naaman the Syrian" (Luke 4:24-27).

For another Christian application of events in the Sister Kingdoms Period see James 5:17-18.

Watershed Event (2 Kings 17)

From 745 to 723 BC the tiny Northern Kingdom tried to maintain its independence from the ever-expanding Assyrian Empire. Some kings paid tribute to the Assyrians; others resisted and came under attack. Thousands of Israelites were deported and resettled in distant lands. Finally the capital of the Northern Kingdom fell to the Assyrians. The former Northern Kingdom was made a province of the Assyrian Empire. The **fall of Samaria in 723 BC** marks the end of the Sister Kingdoms Period.

Summary Chart

S P L I T Kingdom	Biblical Period # 9 SISTER KINGDOM PERIOD 1 Kings 12–2 Kings 17 + 2 Chronicles chs		D E S T R O Y Samaria
	Key Players Jeroboam Ahab Jehu Elijah Elisha Asa Jehoshaphat Joash Jezebel Athaliah	**Major Events** Religion Founded Carmel Meet Jehu Revolt Revivals Attack on David	
931 BC	Duration 208 Years		723 BC

Sister Kingdom Period

Chapter Eleven

Assyrian Period
Brink of Destruction

The Kingdom of Judah survived the destruction of the Northern Kingdom. For the most part during the Assyrian period Judah was a client state of the Assyrian Empire. The Assyrians required enormous tribute. They also required formal recognition of their pagan idols. These were tough days for the people of God. There were, however, two reform movements during this time. You can read the record of the Assyrian Period of Bible history in **2 Kings 18–23**. This material is repeated and supplemented in **2 Chronicles 30–36**. Thus thirteen chapters are devoted to the Assyrian Period.

Duration

The Assyrian Period began with **the conquest of Samaria** by the Assyrian King Shalmaneser in **723 BC**. This period concluded with the Battle of Carchemish in **605 BC**. This means that the Assyrian Period lasted **118 years**.

During this century the world witnessed the ruthless advance of the Assyrian power. By violence, intimidation, and military might the Assyrians built an empire the likes of which the world had never before seen. The great kings of Assyria ruled from the Persian Gulf in the east to the southern borders of Egypt in the west. The Assyrians, however, proved to be better empire builders than empire managers. In the closing years of the Assyrian Period the mighty Assyrian Beast had become a paper tiger.

Scriptural Theme

The following prediction made by the prophet Isaiah foretells the Assyrian invasion of Judah. *The LORD will bring on you and on your people and on the house of your father a time unlike any since Ephraim broke away from Judah – he will bring the king of Assyria"* (Isaiah 7:17). This prophecy was uttered by Isaiah in 734 BC, eleven years before the Assyrians destroyed Samaria, capital of the Northern Kingdom. The prophecy was fulfilled in 701 BC when the powerful King Sennacherib besieged Jerusalem.

Key Players

Six characters are prominent during the Assyrian Period. They can be broken down into three pairs.

Two good kings: **Hezekiah** (*hez-ee-ki´-uh*) was the greatest king since David from the standpoint of his faith (2 Kings 18:5). He led a major reform effort. Hezekiah's life was preserved fifteen extra years so he could lead his people through the crisis of the Assyrian invasion in 701 BC. **Josiah** (*joh-si´-uh*) was the greatest king since the time of David from the standpoint of his works (2 Kings 23:25). He led the final effort to bring Judah back to God. A lost scroll of Scripture was discovered during his reign. Josiah died trying to resist an Egyptian army marching through his land.

Two great prophets: **Isaiah** (*i-zay´-uh*) continued his ministry from the Sister Kingdoms Period. He was the spiritual advisor who helped Hezekiah through the Assyrian invasion in 701 BC. Legend has it that Isaiah died as a martyr by being sawed in two. His large book of sixty-six chapters is full of prophecies about the coming of Christ. **Jeremiah** (*jeh-rih-my´-uh*) came into prominence during the reign of Josiah. He assisted in Josiah's great reformation. Under Josiah's successors he suffered much persecution because of his message. Jeremiah became the dominant figure in Judah for four decades. His large book of fifty-two chapters contains powerful sermons and thrilling stories of how this prophet battled to keep the Judeans faithful to the Lord.

Two tyrants: **King Sennacherib** (*suhn-nak´-uh-rihb*) was the great Assyrian king who invaded Judah in 701 BC. He left in his monuments a record of this invasion. All of Judah and neighboring regions fell to him. In Jerusalem Hezekiah, however, held out, encouraged by the prophet Isaiah. **King Manasseh** (*muh-nas´-seh*) was the worst of the kings of Judah, but also the king who reigned the longest (55 years). Late in his reign Manasseh offended his Assyrian master. He was deported to Babylon in chains. There he repented. God restored him to his throne. Manasseh spent the last years of his life trying to undo the mess he had created as a young man.

Major Events

Here are the five major events of the Assyrian Period:

- ❖ **Hezekiah's revival**
- ❖ **Assyria's invasion**
- ❖ **Manasseh's apostasy**
- ❖ **Josiah's revival**
- ❖ **Nineveh's fall**

Hezekiah's revival (2 Chronicles 29–31). The first thing Hezekiah did when he became king was to open the doors of the temple and repair them (2 Chronicles 29:3). That signaled the beginning of one of the most thoroughgoing religious reforms heretofore undertaken. Pagan shrines were demolished, idols were burned. The national revival culminated in a gigantic Passover celebration. At the end of the prescribed week, the people were on such a spiritual high that they extended the celebration for another seven days. Even some former citizens of the Northern Kingdom came to Jerusalem to join in the festivities. Since the Assyrians required client states to accept their pagan idols, Hezekiah's moves were politically dangerous. He knew that the Assyrians would come to retaliate as soon as they were able.

Invasion (2 Kings 18–19). The anticipated retaliation came when Sennacherib invaded tiny Judah with a massive army. He captured all the outlying cities of Judah and "shut Hezekiah up like a bird in a cage" in Jerusalem, to use the king's own language. Hezekiah received from Sennacherib a letter demanding total surrender. He took the letter to the temple, spread it out before the Lord, and prayed about it. Isaiah the prophet was a strong rock during this crisis. Twice he sent words of encouragement to Hezekiah promising that the Assyrians would never shoot an arrow against Jerusalem. The angel of the Lord entered the Assyrian camp and decimated the mighty army. Sennacherib was forced to retreat to his own land.

Apostasy (2 Kings 21). Judah fell back into the Assyrian orbit of client states after the brief interlude of independence under King Hezekiah. Under King Manasseh paganism and witchcraft were not just tolerated; they were promoted by this king. Pagan altars were even erected in the courtyard of God's temple. Scripture comments: *"Manasseh led them astray, so that they did more evil than the nations the LORD had destroyed before the Israelites"* (2 Kings 21:9). In addition, Manasseh filled the streets of Jerusalem from end to end with innocent blood. This may refer to child sacrifice; it could also refer to the execution of any who opposed the policy of the king. Because of the sins of Manasseh, God announced that Jerusalem must be destroyed.

Josiah's revival (2 Chronicles 34–35). When Manasseh's grandson Josiah came to the throne as a boy, there was temporary improvement in the situation in Jerusalem. Josiah carefully and cautiously began to institute religious reforms, watching for any sign of retaliation from the Assyrians. Josiah's initial tentative steps in reform were bolstered by the preaching of Jeremiah and by the discovery of a long-lost book of God's Law. Ironically, this lost Scripture was found in one of the back chambers of the temple. The royal reforms accelerated. As in the case with the earlier reforms of Hezekiah, Josiah's reform culminated in a great Passover celebration. Not since the days of Samuel had there been a Passover celebration like this.

Fall (Nahum 1–3). The last great Assyrian king was Ashurbanipal (*a´-shuhr-ban´-ih-pal*). When he died in 627 BC, a civil war broke about among rival sons. (Note that the date for the death of the last great Assyrian king coincides with the date for the call of the prophet Jeremiah.) The great empire rapidly began to decline. Even in the heyday of Assyria, Isaiah had foreseen divine judgment on the ruthless Assyrians. The prophet Nahum (*nay´-huhm*) depicted in dramatic fashion the fall of the mighty Assyrian capital of Nineveh (*nihn´-uh-vuhh*) to a foreign conqueror. The prophesied destruction of Nineveh occurred in 612 BC. Remnants of the Assyrian royal family still tried to maintain some semblance of the old empire in other cities. It was plain for all to see, however, that the new power was Babylon (*bab´-ih-lahn*).

Great Miracles

The miracles in the Assyrian Period were few, but rather dramatic. Hezekiah made a miraculous recovery from a terminal illness. Isaiah predicted that the king would live another fifteen years. A sign was offered to bolster the faith of Hezekiah. The shadow went backward ten steps on the royal sun gauge (2 Kings 20:1-11). The miraculous slaughter of a huge number of Assyrian soldiers saved Jerusalem from attack (2 Kings 19:35-36).

God's Message

The outpouring of divine revelation through prophets continued in the Assyrian Period. Besides the two prophets who were key players (**Isaiah; Jeremiah**), four other prophets in this period contributed books to our Bible. These are:

> **Micah** (*mi´-kuh*): *Prophet of Bethlehem's Savior*
> **Nahum:** *Prophet of Nineveh's Doom*
> **Zephaniah** (*zehf-uh-ni´-uh*): *Prophet of God's Wrath*
> **Habakkuk** (*huh-bak´-kuhk*): *Prophet of Faith*

These prophets anticipated the fall of Assyria, the rise of Babylon, the exile of the Judeans, and their return from Babylon. They also predicted the establishment of God's kingdom in the last days.

Christian Application

> *For this reason they could not believe, because, as Isaiah says elsewhere: "He has blinded their eyes and deadened their hearts, so they can neither see with their eyes, nor understand with their hearts, nor turn — and I would heal them." Isaiah said this because he saw Jesus' glory and spoke about him* (John 12:39-41).

The Apostle John attributed prophetic insight to Isaiah. Isaiah is called the Gospel Prophet because of his many predictions regarding Christ and his kingdom. The same can be said of the prophet Micah, who was a contemporary of Isaiah.

Watershed Event (2 Kings 24)

After the fall of Nineveh in 612 BC the Assyrian Empire was shattered. The Egyptians saw the balance of power shifting. Although they were not particularly fond of the Assyrians, they knew that they needed to prop up the remnant of the Assyrian Empire in order to hold Babylon in check. Pharaoh Neco (*nee´-koh*) brought an army northward in 609 BC. He headed for the Euphrates River to aid the Assyrians who were withstanding assaults by the Babylonians.

Assyrian Period

Assyrian Period

For over three years there was a standoff between the Egyptian and Assyrian forces on the one hand, and the Babylonians on the other. Finally near a village named Carchemish (*kahr´-khehm-ihsh*) the two great armies clashed in full battle. It was no contest. The Babylonians crushed the allies. The Egyptians went scurrying southward with the Babylonians in hot pursuit. At the **Battle of Carchemish** in **605 BC** world power changed hands. The Assyrian Period came to an end.

Summary Chart

DESTROY Samaria	Biblical Period # 10 ASSYRIAN PERIOD 1 Kings 18–23 + 2 Chronicles chs		CARCHEMISH Battle
	Key Players Hezekiah Isaiah Manasseh Josiah Jeremiah Sennacherib	**Major Events** Hezekiah Revival Assyrian Invasion Manasseh Apostasy Josiah Revival Nineveh Fall	
723 BC	Duration 118 Years		605 BC

101

Review Time

1. List the four periods of the Patriarchal Age.
2. List the first six periods of the Mosaic Age.
3. In what period would you place . . .
   a. Abraham
   b. Eve
   c. Joshua
   d. Moses
   e. Solomon
   f. Samson
   g. Hezekiah
   h. Jezebel
4. What pivotal character would you place . . .
   a. at about 2000 BC?
   b. at about 1400 BC?
   c. at about 1000 BC?

1. Beginnings, Scattering, Pilgrim, Egyptian
2. Wilderness, Conquest, Judges, Single Kingdom, Sister Kingdoms, Assyrian.
3. a. Pilgrim; b. Beginnings; c. Conquest; d. Egyptian; Wilderness; e. Single Kingdom; f. Judges; g. Assyrian; h. Sister Kingdoms.
4. a. Abraham; b. Moses; c. David.

Assyrian Period

Chapter Twelve

BABYLONIAN PERIOD
Deportation and Desolation

For a number of years Jeremiah had warned Judah about an enemy from the north. Habakkuk had also indicated that God would bring the wicked Chaldeans against Judah to punish the nation. Shortly after the Battle of Carchemish in 605 BC it became clear that these were no idle threats.

The pursuit of the Egyptian forces southward brought the Babylonian army to Jerusalem. Josiah's son Jehoiakim was now ruling. He was put in chains to be deported to Babylon (2 Chronicles 36:6). For some reason Nebuchadnezzar, the Babylonian commander, decided to leave Jehoiakim on the throne. The Judean king was forced to take an oath of allegiance to the conquerors. Members of the royal family were deported to Babylon as hostages. Among them were Daniel, Shadrach, Meshach, and Abednego.

The historical information concerning the Babylonian Period must be pieced together from **snippets in 2 Kings 24, Daniel, Jeremiah, and Ezekiel**.

Duration

The Babylonian Period began with the Battle of Carchemish in 605 BC. At that battle Nebuchadnezzar became the master of the world. His reign of forty-seven years was a glorious period for

Babylon. Not only was Nebuchadnezzar a brilliant military strategist, he was also a great builder. After his death, however, the Babylonian Empire experienced rapid deterioration. In 539 BC the Persian King Cyrus conquered Babylon virtually without battle. So the Babylonian Period lasted from 605 to 539 BC, **67 years**.

Scriptural Theme

> *This is what the* LORD *Almighty, the God of Israel, says to all those I carried into exile from Jerusalem to Babylon: "Build houses and settle down; plant gardens and eat what they produce. . . . When seventy years are completed for Babylon, I will come to you and fulfill my gracious promise to bring you back to this place"* (Jeremiah 29:4, 5, 10).

These words were part of a letter sent by Jeremiah to the Jews that were held captive in Babylon. Those captives were being told by false prophets that their captivity would not last long. Jeremiah, however, advised the captives to settle down in Babylon. They were going to be there for seventy years. Only after seventy years of Babylonian world power would any Jews return to Palestine.

Key Players

Four main characters surface in the Babylonian period. These can be displayed in two categories:

Bible prophets: **Daniel** (*dan´-iehl*) was taken hostage to Babylon early in the Babylonian Period. There he was selected for training in the royal academies (Daniel 1). He served in the administration of Nebuchadnezzar. During that time Daniel began to exercise his gift of dream interpretation (Daniel 2, 4). As an old man Daniel surfaced again in the last days of Babylon to interpret some mysterious handwriting on the wall of the royal palace (Daniel 5).

Ezekiel (*e-zee´-kih-ehl*) arrived in Babylon eight years after Daniel. He preached to the thousands of Jews in Babylon who were discouraged and homesick. Ezekiel was famous for the many antics that he performed to illustrate his sermons. For example, once he shaved off all his hair in public. He then used the hair to illustrate what was going to happen to the Jews who were still living back in Jerusalem.

Babylonian kings: **Nebuchadnezzar** (*neh-bew-kad-nehz´-zuhr*) started his career as the leader of the army. When his father died, he was made king. He ruled for forty-seven years. He is famous for building the Hanging Gardens of Babylon, one of the seven wonders of the ancient world. In the Bible Nebuchadnezzar had two dreams that revealed his future and the future of the world (Daniel 2, 4). Daniel interpreted the dreams for the king. God humbled Nebuchadnezzar when for seven years he lived with the animals and ate grass like an ox (Daniel 4).

Belshazzar (*bel-shaz´-ahr*) was ruling in Babylon at the time the city was captured. God revealed to the king and his banquet guests that the city was about to be given over to the Persians. Daniel was brought out of retirement to read the mysterious prediction etched on the palace wall (Daniel 5). Belshazzar was slain on the night Cyrus's army conquered Babylon.

Major Events

Five major events took place during the Babylonian Period.

- ❖ **Jews deported**
- ❖ **Ezekiel called**
- ❖ **Jeremiah persecuted**
- ❖ **Jerusalem destroyed**
- ❖ **Nebuchadnezzar humbled**

Deportation *(2 Kings 24:12-17).* After three years King Jehoiakim (*jih-hoy´-uh-kihm*) broke his oath to Nebuchadnezzar and rebelled against him. By the time Nebuchadnezzar arrived at Jerusalem to punish him, Jehoiakim had died. Jehoiakim's eighteen-year-old son with a similar sounding name (Jehoiachin) was ruling. The young king held out against Nebuchadnezzar for three months or so. Then he decided to surrender. King Jehoiachin (*jih-hoy´-uh-kin*) and 10,000 leading citizens of Jerusalem were deported in chains to Babylon. Among those captives was Ezekiel. Nebuchadnezzar also took many of the golden temple vessels to Babylon. He put them in the temple of his god as trophies of triumph over the God of the Jews.

Call *(Ezekiel 1–3)*. After Ezekiel had been in Babylon for five years, God called him to be his spokesman to the captives there. The call was the most dramatic in the Bible. Ezekiel saw a vision of a throne being transported by four living creatures, each of whom had four wings and four faces. On the throne he saw a vision (remember the word theophany?) of God. God handed Ezekiel a scroll and told him to eat it. (In dreams and visions prophets did strange things.) The scroll represented God's message to the Jews in Babylon.

Persecution *(Jeremiah 26–38)*. During the last twenty years of his ministry Jeremiah experienced intense persecution by the rulers of Jerusalem and the religious establishment. There were plots against his life by neighbors in his hometown, and later by the authorities. The prophet was beaten, thrown into subterranean prisons, and left in a pit to die. During the months when the Babylonians were besieging Jerusalem, Jeremiah was confined in the court of the guard. He lived through the three-year siege of Jerusalem. After Jerusalem was destroyed, Jeremiah was kidnapped by his own people and forced to go to Egypt.

Jerusalem destroyed *(2 Kings 25)*. The last Jewish king of the Old Testament was Zedekiah, the third son of Josiah to sit on the throne. Toward the end of his eleven-year reign Zedekiah rebelled against Nebuchadnezzar. The army of Babylon came in force against the city again. The Babylonians broke through the walls and captured Zedekiah. Then they dismantled and burned the city. More Jews were then deported to Babylon to join the thousands that already had been deported there. For several years Jerusalem was uninhabited and in ruins. This important date in Bible history was 586 BC.

Nebuchadnezzar humbled *(Daniel 4)*. Because Nebuchadnezzar had become so haughty, God decided to humble him. He revealed his intentions to the king in a dream, which Daniel interpreted for him. The king was being given an opportunity to repent. By the end of the year there was no indication of humility. So God inflicted upon the great king the mentality of an animal. For seven years Nebuchadnezzar was literally put out to pasture. When he turned his eyes heavenward and acknowledged the Living God, his sanity was restored.

Great Miracles

Aside from the amazing prophecies of Daniel (see under God's Message), the Book of Daniel records one great miracle that God performed among the captives during the Babylonian Period. That is the miracle of the **fiery furnace** (Daniel 3). Generally speaking the Jews in Babylon had religious freedom. There was one occasion, however, when the proud Nebuchadnezzar ordered all his subjects to worship a giant golden image which he had erected. Three Hebrew young men—Shadrach, Meshach, and Abednego—refused to obey the command. They were thrown into a furnace of fire. The fire, however, did not harm them. Nebuchadnezzar saw a fourth "man" walking about with them in the furnace. The Lord was standing with his servants in their hour of trial. This incident impressed the Babylonian king with the greatness of the God of the Jews.

God's Message

Besides the books of **Jeremiah, Ezekiel** and **Daniel,** the **Book of Lamentations** also was written during the Babylonian Period. It gives an eyewitness account of the destruction of Jerusalem by

Nebuchadnezzar in poetic lines. It is hard to isolate specific prophecies as the most important revelation of this period, but here is one prophecy from each of the three great prophets of the period that illustrates their ministries.

- ❖ **Jeremiah's new covenant prophecy**
- ❖ **Ezekiel's dry bones vision**
- ❖ **Daniel's world empire outline**

New covenant (Jeremiah 31:31-32). Jeremiah foresaw the Christian Age, the days of the new covenant. The new covenant envisioned by Jeremiah was not based on commandments written in stone. God's commandments were to be written on the hearts of his people. Jesus instituted that new covenant when he died on the cross and rose from the dead.

Dry Bones (Ezekiel 37). Ezekiel in a vision saw a valley full of bones. God explained that these bones represented the Israelites in captivity. As a nation they were dead, dry, and disjointed. Their situation seemed to be hopeless. Yet Ezekiel saw the bones coming back together, forming skeletons. He saw skin coming over them. The corpses rose to their feet. Then God breathed his life into them. They rose as a mighty army. God explained that Israel would be restored to life and to their land. We will see how these predictions were fulfilled during the next period of Bible history.

World empires (Daniel 2, 7). Daniel's prophecy of the four world empires appears in two formats. In Daniel 2 the four empires are represented by the golden head, the silver chest, the bronze belly and the iron legs of a giant image. In Daniel 7 the empires are compared to a lion with wings, a lopsided bear, a four-headed leopard, and a beast totally different from anything in nature. The first empire is identified as Babylon. The other three world empires are Persia, Greece, and Rome. In the days of those kings God was to set up his own kingdom, one that was to endure forever. The kingdom envisioned by Daniel is Christ's kingdom that is not of this world. On earth his kingdom is represented by the church.

Babylonian Period

Christian Application

Jesus used the predictions of Daniel to warn his disciples to flee Jerusalem lest they be caught up in the Roman siege of the city. *"So when you see standing in the holy place 'the abomination that causes desolation,' spoken of through the prophet Daniel* [Daniel 9:27; 11:31; 12:11] *– let the reader understand – then let those who are in Judea flee to the mountains"* (Matthew 24:15-16). Jerusalem Christians heeded this warning from Jesus. The initial assault against Jerusalem by the Romans was repulsed by the Jews. The Christians took the opportunity to flee from the city. Thousands of Jews, however, took refuge in Jerusalem behind the massive walls. When the Romans returned in larger numbers, they leveled Jerusalem. The carnage and loss of life was unimaginable. Not one Christian, however, is known to have lost his life in the destruction of Jerusalem in AD 70.

Watershed Event (Daniel 5)

After Nebuchadnezzar's death in 562 BC a series of inept rulers occupied the throne of Babylon. By 550 BC a new power was arising in the east. Cyrus the Persian was starting a march of conquest that brought him to the gates of Babylon in October 539 BC. Using a stratagem to gain entrance into the city, the troops of Cyrus overwhelmed Babylon facing only token resistance from the defenders. With the **fall of Babylon in 539 BC** the era of Babylonian world rule came to an end.

Summary Chart

C A R C H E M I S H Battle	Biblical Period # 11 BABYLONIAN PERIOD 2 Kings 24 + Daniel, Jeremiah, Ezekiel chs		F A L L Babylon
	Key Players Daniel Ezekiel Nebuchadnezzar Belshazzar	**Major Events** Jews Deported Ezekiel Called Jeremiah Persecuted Jerusalem Destroyed Nebuchadnezzar Humbled	
605 BC	Duration 67 Years		539 BC

Babylonian Period

Chapter Thirteen

Persian Period
Restoration and Reconstruction

The Assyrians and Babylonians tried to control subject peoples with intimidation, brutality and religious oppression. The Persians had a different philosophy. Under the Persians captive peoples had a great amount of religious freedom. The government encouraged and even aided the rebuilding of religious shrines. With the Babylonian exile at an end the people of God were given the opportunity of returning to their native land. One can read the record of the Persian or Postexilic period in the books of **Ezra, Nehemiah, and Esther**. Thirty-three chapters of Scriptures are devoted to this period.

Duration

The Persian period began with the conquest of Babylon by Cyrus in 539 BC. Politically the Persian Empire was overthrown by Alexander the Great in 332 BC. Bible history, however, comes to an end with the second governorship of Nehemiah in 432 BC. This is the last concrete date of Old Testament history. To accommodate the years of Nehemiah's second governorship we shall extend the date of the Persian Period to 400 BC. So in round figures the Persian Period extends from 539 to 400 BC — about **139 years**.

Scriptural Theme

"Now these are the people of the province who came up from the captivity of the exiles, whom Nebuchadnezzar king of Babylon had taken captive to Babylon (they returned to Jerusalem and Judah, each to his own town)" (Ezra 2:1). This verse captures the essence of what transpired during the final period of Old Testament history. Jewish exiles were permitted to return home to rebuild their land. Former captives trickled back throughout the period; but there are two recorded large-scale migrations of captives.

Key Players

Four of the five Persian kings who reigned between 539–432 BC are mentioned in the Scriptures: Cyrus, Darius, Xerxes, and Artaxerxes. Three great enemies of the Jews surfaced during this period: Haman (in Persia) and Sanballat and Tobiah (in Palestine). There were three great prophets of God during the Persian Period: Haggai, Zechariah, and Malachi. The action in the Persian Period, however, revolves around five main characters:

- ❖ **Zerubbabel the governor**
- ❖ **Joshua the high priest**
- ❖ **Esther the queen**
- ❖ **Ezra the scribe**
- ❖ **Nehemiah the builder**

Governor. The first contingent of Jews to return from Babylon to Judea was led by **Zerubbabel** (*zeh-ruhb´-buh-behl*). He was a descendant of David. Perhaps for that reason Zerubbabel was appointed by the Persians to be the first governor of the Persian province of Judea. Zerubbabel was a great man of faith. He was encouraged in his leadership by the prophets Haggai (*hag´-gi*) and Zechariah (*zehk-uh-ri´-uh*). The lasting monument to Zerubbabel's leadership was the rebuilding of the Jerusalem temple which was completed in 516 BC.

Persian Period

High priest. The first high priest after the return from exile was named **Joshua** (*jah´-shew-uh*). Special messages in Haggai and Zechariah are addressed to this man. Joshua the high priest is regarded as a picture or preview of Christ our great high priest.

Queen. A Jewish girl named **Esther** (*ehs´-tuhr*) was selected to be queen of the Persian Empire during the days of King Xerxes (*zerk´-seez*). She was able to use her influence with the king to thwart a plot to wipe out the Jews throughout the Persian Empire. Though she was not a particularly religious person, God placed her in high position so that she might rescue his people from extermination.

Scribe. **Ezra** (*ehz´-ruh*) was a scribe (scholar) and priest. He was appointed to supervise Jewish affairs in a large region of the Persian Empire. He discovered that some Jewish men had married foreign wives who worshiped idols. Ezra effectively dealt with this problem. Apparently Ezra also attempted to rebuild the walls of Jerusalem (Ezra 4:6-23). For this action he had no authorization. Enemies of the Jews notified the king. The king fired back an edict that permitted the enemies to dismantle the work that had been done on the walls. Many of the Jews lost faith in Ezra.

Builder. **Nehemiah** (*nee-huh-mi´-uh*) was a cupbearer to the Persian king. In 445 BC Nehemiah's king permitted him to return to Judea as governor. He had a mandate to rebuild Jerusalem's walls. In spite of intense opposition, Nehemiah succeeded in building the walls. He then drafted citizens to repopulate the city. After thirteen years Nehemiah returned to Persia to have his commission renewed. His second governorship in Jerusalem commenced in 432 BC.

Major Events

Five events rise to a level of importance that merits listing here. These are:

- ❖ First return
- ❖ Temple rebuilt
- ❖ Genocide thwarted
- ❖ Reforms enforced
- ❖ Walls rebuilt

First return (Ezra 1–3). When Cyrus (*si´-rus*) conquered Babylon, he liberated all captive peoples, including the Jews. God's people were permitted to return home in 538 BC. They were given permission to rebuild their temple. The Jews took with them the temple vessels that had been taken to Babylon by Nebuchadnezzar. Those who returned numbered about 42,000+ heads of families, or about 200,000 people. Many Jews elected to remain in the lands of the captivity where they were prospering. Those who did return were spiritually minded. This contingent of Jews was led by Zerubbabel.

Temple rebuilt (Ezra 4–6). The first thing the returnees did when they got back was to build an altar at which they could worship God. They laid the foundations for the temple. They gathered materials for the task. Then harassment by enemies and a series of crop failures created discouragement. The work ceased. For over a decade no further work on the temple was done. The wood that had been gathered for the temple gradually disappeared. (Mysteriously wood paneling began to show up in the homes of people.) Zerubbabel and Joshua could not muster any workers for the project. Then God raised up two prophets who preached so powerfully that the work resumed in a matter of days. Four years after the work was renewed, the structure — referred to as Zerubbabel's temple — was completed.

Genocide thwarted (Esther). In distant Persia a Prime Minster named Haman developed a personal grudge against a Jew named Mordecai. The king was in need of finances; so Haman offered him an enormous sum for permitting him to slay all the Jews. Haman was to retain for himself the spoils of every Jewish family in the empire. Mordecai pressed Queen Esther to get involved. She used her influence to get the king to issue a counter edict encouraging Jews to defend themselves on the appointed day. The king ordered Haman to be hung for trying to deceive him.

Reforms enforced *(Ezra 7-10).* In the seventh year of King Artaxerxes (457 BC) a scholar and priest named Ezra led another contingent of Jews home from the lands of exile. The king authorized Ezra to enforce the Law of God throughout the region west of the Euphrates River. Ezra was informed that many Jewish men had married foreign women. Children were being raised who could not even speak the language of the Jews. Ezra organized a national assembly that authorized a divorce court. This divorce court traveled from village to village investigating every alleged violation of God's marriage law. The men were ordered to put away their pagan wives, unless the women had committed themselves to the Lord. The divorce court found 111 cases where action needed to be taken.

Walls rebuilt *(Nehemiah 1-12).* In the twentieth year of Artaxerxes, Nehemiah received news in the Persian capital that the walls of Jerusalem were again in ruins. His king gave him permission to go to Jerusalem and rebuild the walls. Nehemiah received a twelve-year appointment as governor of Judea. The new governor faced opposition from the Gentile neighbors of the Jews. They tried every form of intimidation, including the threat of force, to halt the work. Nehemiah, however, had the reconstruction effort so well organized that within fifty-two days the wall was completed.

Great Miracles

Only one miracle is recorded in the Persian Period, and that right at the beginning (Daniel 6). Most of the ministry of Daniel occurred in the Babylonian Period. His ministry, however, extended into the earliest years of the Persian Empire. Daniel had a high position in the government of King Darius who ruled in Babylon.

Political enemies tricked the king into issuing an edict that anyone who made a petition to any god or man (other than the king) for a month was to be thrown into a lions' den. The king was flattered. He signed the edict. Daniel was not a defiant man; but he did not let the king's decree prevent him from praying three times a day facing in the direction of Jerusalem. Daniel was arrested. Much to the regret of the king, he was thrown into a lions' den. Darius rushed to the den early in the morning. There Daniel was found unharmed. Those who had tricked the king into signing the edict were themselves thrown to the lions. The hungry beasts snatched them out of the air before they even hit the floor. Darius was so impressed that he was moved to praise the God of the Jews.

God's Message

Three complete prophetic books come out of the Persian Period, plus certain chapters of the Book of Daniel. **Daniel** prophetically outlined events leading to the establishment of Messiah's kingdom. He made specific predictions about the "last days" of Old Testament times and the appearance of the Messiah (Daniel 9–12).

The prophet **Haggai** focused on getting the temple rebuilt. He also announced a great shake-up that was to result in the establishment of Christ's kingdom.

Zechariah the prophet rose up to support the preaching of Haggai. He recorded a series of visions that depict God's relationship with his people from Zechariah's day to the final judgment. The last six chapters of his book are full of prophecies of events that were to transpire between the Old Testament and the New Testament. These chapters also contain many specific prophecies about the coming of Christ.

Malachi (*mal´-uh-ki*) was the last prophet of the Old Testament. He focused on worship which had become formal and cold. Malachi foresaw the day when spiritual worship would be offered to the Lord throughout the world. Malachi closes the Old

Testament with the announcement that a messenger was to come who would proclaim a new covenant.

Christian Application

When Jesus announced in Galilee *the time is fulfilled*, he may have been referencing the prophecy in Daniel 9:24-27. Jesus' reference to praying a mountain into the sea (Matthew 17:20; 21:21) may be an application of Zechariah 4:7. The reference is to a mountain of opposition standing in the path of God's work. The writer of Hebrews quotes from Haggai:

> *At that time* [Mount Sinai] *his voice shook the earth, but now he has promised, "Once more I will shake not only the earth but also the heavens." The words "once more" indicate the removing of what can be shaken—that is, created things—so that what cannot be shaken may remain. Therefore, since we are receiving a kingdom that cannot be shaken, let us be thankful* (Hebrews 12:26-29a).

So the writer of the Book of Hebrews regarded the Church Age as the fulfillment of the prophecies of Haggai about an unshakable kingdom.

Watershed Event (Nehemiah 13)

The last event of the Old Testament is recorded in Nehemiah 13. Nehemiah returned from a visit to the Persian capital with a reappointment to the governorship. During that time Nehemiah corrected Sabbath abuse, rebuked intermarriage with pagan wives and oversaw the purification of the priesthood. He discovered that during his absence, the major enemy of the Jews had been given a room in the courts of the temple. Nehemiah threw him out. How long Nehemiah lived after his second appointment cannot be determined. A good round figure date for the conclusion of his life is 400 BC. The death of Nehemiah marks the end of the Persian Period of Old Testament history.

Summary Chart

F A L L Babylon	Biblical Period # 12 PERSIAN PERIOD Ezra, Nehemiah, Esther		D E A T H Nehemiah
	Key Players Zerubbabel Joshua Esther Ezra Nehemiah	**Major Events** First Return Temple Rebuilt Genocide Thwarted Reforms Enforced Walls Rebuilt	
539 BC	**Duration:** 139 Years		400 BC

Persian Period

Chapter Fourteen

Silent Period
Countdown to Christ

The last recorded event in the Old Testament took place in the 32nd year of the Persian King Artaxerxes (Nehemiah 13:6). On our dating system this equates to 432 BC. That was when Nehemiah returned to Jerusalem to resume his governorship. So the second governorship of Nehemiah is the last recorded event of the Old Testament.

The period following the close of the Old Testament might be called the *Greek Period*, because the dominating culture was that of the Greeks. Some refer to these centuries as the *Intertestamental Period* because this is the period between the close of the Old Testament and the opening of the New Testament. The designation *Silent Period* reminds us that God did not speak through prophets during these centuries. Nothing new was added to the revelation of God.

Some might question whether a chapter on this period should be included in a book dealing with Bible history. The inclusion is justified, however, for two reasons. First, there is a good deal of predictive material in the Old Testament that was fulfilled during the Silent Period. Second, the Silent Period forms the background for the New Testament. Understanding what went on in this period will assist in understanding the Christian Scriptures.

Duration

Scripture does not indicate how long the second governorship of Nehemiah lasted. If he served a full twelve-year term, that would bring the conclusion of Old Testament history to 420 BC. For the purposes of this simplified overview, however, we arbitrarily have designated 400 BC as the termination point for Old Testament history. So the Silent Period began about 400 BC. This period ended with the announcements of the births of John the Baptist and Jesus about 6 BC.

Some are confused about how Jesus could be born in the era that we label BC. The system of numbering years AD (for *Anno Domini*) was instituted in about the year AD 527 by the Roman abbot Dionysius Exiguus. This monk reckoned that the birth announcement for Jesus occurred on March 25 in the year 754 AUC (Latin for *from the founding of Rome*) with the birth of Jesus occurring nine months later. Thus the year 754 AUC was designated by him as the year AD 1. Bede, the eighth-century English historian, began the practice of counting years backward from AD 1. In this system, the year AD 1 is preceded by the year 1 BC, without an intervening year 0.

The New Testament requires that Jesus was born before the death of Herod the Great. Herod died in 4 BC. Today scholars generally agree that Jesus was born between 6 and 4 BC. Obviously the birth announcement to Mary came nine months earlier. The birth announcement to John's father was six months earlier still.

The Silent Period lasted from about 400 to 6 BC, or roughly **400 years**.

Theme Scripture

The prophet Zechariah foresaw the mighty struggle between God's people and the Greeks during the Silent Period. *"I will bend Judah as I bend my bow and fill it with Ephraim. I will rouse your sons, O Zion, against your sons, O Greece, and make you like a warrior's sword"* (Zechariah 9:13).

Key Players

Among the leading characters of the Silent Period are two Greek kings, three Jewish leaders, and a king appointed by Rome.

- ❖ **Alexander the Great**
- ❖ **Antiochus Epiphanes**
- ❖ **Judas Maccabeus**
- ❖ **Simon Maccabeus**
- ❖ **John Hyrcanus**
- ❖ **Herod the Great**

Greek kings. **Alexander the Great** (356–323 BC) was one of the greatest military leaders of history. He destroyed the Persian Empire. He spread Greek language and culture by founding Greek cities all over the Near East. This culture still dominated the scene when Christ came into the world. The rise and fall of Alexander was prophesied by Daniel. Alexander is depicted as the notable horn on a shaggy goat (the Greek Empire) in Daniel 8:21.

The second Greek king who is a key player in this period is **Antiochus** (*an-ti´-ah-khuhs* **Epiphanes** (*eh-pif´-ah-nees*) who ruled Syria and controlled Palestine 175–163 BC. Twice he attacked the Greek king who ruled Egypt. On one of those occasions the Romans intervened and thwarted his advance. Retracing his steps through Palestine, Antiochus took out his frustration on the Jews. A terrible persecution broke out. Antiochus is the little horn whose appearance is predicted in Daniel 8:9; he is the *contemptible person* in the prophecy of Daniel 11:21.

Jewish leaders. The first outstanding Jewish leader in the Silent Period was **Judas Maccabeus** (*mak-kah-bee´-uhs*). He became leader of a guerrilla army during the persecution by Antiochus (166–160 BC). *Maccabeus* is a nickname meaning *hammer*. Time and again Judas fought against Greek armies many times the size of his own force. After about three years Judas was able to retake Jerusalem from the Greeks.

Simon Maccabeus (142–135 BC) was the brother of Judas. About 141 BC Simon secured from the Greek ruler freedom from taxation for the Jewish people. At last the Jews had achieved political freedom. Simon was acclaimed by the people as their leader and high priest forever. The high priests hereafter traced their ancestry back to Aaron through Simon. He founded a dynasty of rulers. The dynasty is called the Hasmonean (*hahs-moh-nee´-ahn*) dynasty, named after a distant ancestor of Simon.

John Hyrcanus (134–104 BC). Hyrcanus (*hear´-kan-uhs*) was high priest and civil ruler of the Jews. He expanded the territory of the Jews in all directions. Peoples in those regions were forced to convert to Judaism or move elsewhere.

Herod the Great (37–4 BC). Herod was appointed by the Romans to be "king of the Jews" even though he was not of Jewish heritage. He engaged in great building projects all over Palestine including cities, harbors, and fortresses. He is perhaps most famous for his elaborate remodeling and enlargement of the Jerusalem temple. Herod was ruthless in dealing with enemies. He executed members of his own family because he was suspicious of their intentions. Herod was threatened by reports of some travelers from the east. He ordered his soldiers to kill all the infants in Bethlehem under the age of two. Herod seems to be the king prophetically described in Daniel 11:36-45.

Major Events

Five events are of special importance in the Silent Period.

- ❖ **Alexander's conquests**
- ❖ **Translation of Scripture**
- ❖ **Persecution of Jews**
- ❖ **Cleansing of Temple**
- ❖ **Invasion by the Romans**

Conquests. At the age of twenty-two Alexander led a comparatively small Greek army into territories of the Persian Empire.

Silent Period

His purpose was to repay the Persians for two recent invasions of Greece. In 334 BC Alexander led his troops into Asia Minor (modern Turkey) where they won a series of victories over the Persians. The victorious march continued into Syria and Egypt. From victories there, Alexander led his troops into Persia, Media, and as far east as northern India. Legend has it that at that point he wept, for there were no more worlds to conquer. The truth is that his army refused to go any further east. On the return trip to Greece Alexander passed through Babylon, where he died in 323 BC at the age of thirty-three.

Alexander's most lasting legacy was his spread of Greek culture. Everywhere he went, he tried to instill that culture. The process of spreading Greek culture is called *Hellenization*. This process included especially the Greek language, schools, and emphasis on athletic competition. The gymnasium was the center of a Greek city. Unfortunately several of the Jewish high priests became so Hellenized that they basically were Greeks in Jewish clothing. Reports exist that some Jewish men were undergoing surgery to reverse their circumcision so they would not be identified as Jews when they competed (in the nude) in athletic contests.

Translation. One of the Greek rulers of Egypt had an obsession to build a library that would house every book that had ever been written. He was told about the Hebrew Scriptures. Jewish scholars were summoned to Alexandria, Egypt, to translate the Hebrew Scriptures into the Greek language. This took place about 250 BC. This translation is called today the *Septuagint* (*sehp-tew´-uh-gihnt*) — *the Seventy* — abbreviated LXX. It gets its name from the seventy scholars who were responsible for the translation. This translation in the international language of the day made the message of the Old Testament available to a wider audience. Later Paul found Greek-speaking believers in virtually every synagogue. They became a fertile field for the gospel seed that Paul planted.

Persecution. In 168 BC Antiochus Epiphanes tried to bring unity to his kingdom by declaring himself a god. Everyone was required to pay homage. Most Jews refused. This brought down the wrath of Antiochus upon the Jewish people. The Jerusalem temple was seized and desecrated. A pagan altar was erected in the temple courtyard. Daniel predicted this persecution. He talked about a horn (Antiochus) on a goat (the Greek Empire) that *"grew until it reached the host of the heavens"* (God's people). Then it *"threw some of the starry host down to the earth and trampled on them"* (Daniel 8:10). John may be looking back on this persecution when he spoke of a great red dragon (Satan) sweeping down a third of the stars out of the sky and flinging them to the earth just before the Christ child was born (Revelation 12:4). So the persecution by Antiochus was Satan's attempt to destroy the people of God.

Cleansing. Three years after Antiochus desecrated the temple, Judas Maccabeus retook Jerusalem. The year was 165 BC. The Jews cleansed the temple. They resumed worship to the Lord. This cleansing of the temple is still celebrated by the Jews in the Feast of Hanukkah (*chahn´-nook-kaw*) each December.

Invasion. In 63 BC the Roman General Pompey conquered Jerusalem. Pompey slew 12,000 Jews who defended their temple. Pompey expected to see some wonderful sight in the Holy of Holies of the temple. All he found was a slab of stone upon which the high priests sprinkled the blood of the sacrificial goat on the Day of Atonement. The beautiful and valuable Ark of the Covenant, that had been in the Holy of Holies in Solomon's time, had been lost or destroyed when the Babylonians conquered Jerusalem in 586 BC. The invasion by Pompey marked the beginning of the Roman occupation of Palestine that was in place when Jesus was born in the days of Caesar Augustus (Luke 2:1). The Romans ruled Palestine through procurators (governors appointed by the Roman emperor) and puppet kings.

Great Miracles

The Jewish books that were written during the Silent Period contain accounts of supernatural events, sometimes ludicrous, sometimes eerie. Of the ludicrous variety is the story in the Book of Tobit. In this tale fish guts were used to drive demons out of a wedding chamber, and to heal the eyes of a blind man. An example of the eerie variety of miracle is what is supposed to have happened when a Greek general forced his way into the temple. A supernatural horseman attired in golden armor attacked him. At the same time two supernatural young men appeared who beat the general with whips until he lay in a heap on the ground speechless and motionless. Sacrifices by the high priest caused the two supernatural young men to return to tell the general to be grateful to the high priest for intervening to save his life (2 Macc 3:22-34). The book of 2 Maccabees is full of miraculous signs and interventions by angels.

There is some reason to question whether any of these stories are true. They read like legend rather than history. The more sober history of the same period is 1 Maccabees, which records nothing that seems supernatural. It is probably safe to say that there are no documented miracles during the Silent Period.

God's Message

The Jews living in the Silent Period realized that the Holy Spirit of prophecy had departed from Israel (1 Macc 4:45f; 9:27; Song of the Three Holy Children v 15; Josephus *Against Apion*, 1.8; Talmud, *Sanhedrin* 11a). So there were no books of Scripture written during this period.

Several books written during the Silent Period, however, were highly valued among some early Christians. Fourteen books (or parts of books) are known collectively as the *Apocrypha* (among Protestants) and *Deutero-canonical* books (among Roman Catholics). Here is a breakdown of those books, along with a brief description of the contents of each. The books in bold type are included in Roman Catholic Bibles. The others are regarded by Catholics as an appendix to the New Testament that is frequently not printed.

History books. Three of the books of the Apocrypha are classified as history books. The book called **1 Maccabees** is a fairly reliable history of the Jews between 175–135 BC. **2 Maccabees** focuses on the Greek persecution of the Jews and the exploits of Judas Maccabeus in the period 175–160 BC. 1 Esdras is the biblical history of Ezra–Nehemiah retold with one fanciful story about Zerubbabel (builder of the second temple) inserted.

Romance books. A *romance* is a tale depicting heroic or marvelous achievements, colorful events, unusual experiences, or other matters that appeal to the imagination. **Tobit** is a well-written short story about a Jewish young man who possessed some magical fish guts by which he drove a demon from the marriage chamber of a bride, and healed the eyes of his blind father. **Judith** is the story of a Jewish woman who used her beauty and wiles to decapitate the commander of an enemy force attacking her village.

Prophetic books. Three books of the Apocrypha are classified as prophetic. **Baruch** offers reflections on life under foreign rulers, a poem on wisdom, and a poetic lament over Jerusalem. The **Epistle of Jeremiah** purports to be a copy of the letter that Jeremiah sent to the captives in Babylon in 597 BC. It is actually more of a sermon ridiculing idolatry than a letter. In Catholic Bibles this "book" usually is attached to the Book of Baruch. 2 Esdras contains seven highly symbolic visions similar to those in the Book of Revelation dealing with the mysteries of the moral world.

Additions to books. The Apocrypha contains certain chapters that in the Catholic Bible are integrated into two biblical books. The Greek **Additions to Esther** are inserted at six points in the Hebrew Book of Esther in order to increase the religious content of the book. There are three additions to Daniel. The **Prayer of Azariah and Song of the Three Hebrew Children** consists of sixty-eight poetic verses loosely related to the episode of the fiery furnace in Daniel 3. **Bel and the Dragon** consists of two well-written short stories about how Daniel proved that the Babylonian gods were lifeless and harmless. **Susanna** is the story of a beautiful Jewish woman who is falsely accused of adultery (a capital crime) by two lecherous judges. The judges are exposed and executed as a result of clever cross examination by Daniel.

Silent Period

Wisdom books. Two of the books of the Apocrypha are classified as wisdom books. **Ecclesiasticus** (*ek-klee-zee-as´-tih-kus*) is a long book (48 chs.) containing moral and religious proverbs occasionally expanded into short essays. A writer pretending to be Solomon reflects on the meaning of history, life after death, and the glories of wisdom in the **Wisdom of Solomon**.

Christian Application

The New Testament does not directly quote from the books written in the Silent Period. Neither Jesus nor the apostles regarded the books of the Apocrypha as Scripture. There may be an allusion to the tortures inflicted upon the Jews during persecution by Antiochus Epiphanes in Hebrews 11:35 (see 2 Maccabees 7). As noted above, John may have been depicting this same persecution in the symbolism of Revelation 12:1-4. The Christian application from the Silent Period is best captured in this verse by the Apostle Paul: *"But when the time had fully come, God sent his Son, born of a woman, born under law, to redeem those under law, that we might receive the full rights of sons"* (Galatians 4:4f).

The Silent Period contains historical developments that were crucial to the successful launching of the Christian faith. The Romans controlled the Mediterranean world. They built 250,000 miles of highways connecting far distant regions with Rome. The roads facilitated travel, which in turn facilitated the spread of the gospel. The Roman navy patrolled the sea lanes, protecting shipping from outlaws. This too contributed to Christian missionary travel. The Roman era was characterized by peace known as the *pax Romana*. There was a universal language (Greek) that facilitated communication wherever Christians went preaching the gospel. Through the Septuagint (Greek) Old Testament, teaching about the one true God and the hope of a coming Messiah had spread to the farthest corner of the Roman Empire. Among the Gentiles there was growing rejection of the old pagan religions. This made Gentiles more receptive to the new ideas of Christianity. All of these factors indicate that Jesus was born at just the right time to have a maximum impact on his world.

Watershed Event

The Silent Period ended with two birth announcements about 6 BC. The first of these preceded the birth of Jesus by fifteen months. An old priest Zechariah and his wife Elizabeth were a godly couple. They had no children. During his priestly duties in Jerusalem Zechariah entered the temple to burn incense. The angel Gabriel appeared to him to announce that he and his wife would have a son. The son was to be named John. His ministry was to prepare the way for the Messiah (Luke 1:8-20).

Six months later the same angel appeared to Mary, a Jewish maiden who lived in Nazareth. She was engaged to Joseph, a local carpenter. The angel told Mary that she was expecting a special child who had been conceived by the Holy Spirit. This child was to become great. He was to sit on the throne of David his ancestor (Luke 1:26-38).

When Joseph realized that his wife-to-be was pregnant he was prepared to break off the engagement. In those days breaking an engagement required legal action similar to divorce. The angel Gabriel, however, appeared also to Joseph. He was informed about the circumstances of the baby's conception. The angel urged Joseph to marry the maiden. When the child was born, he was to be given the name *Jesus*, which means *Savior* (Matthew 1:18-25). The birth announcements of John and Jesus marked the end of the Silent Period.

Silent Period

Summary Chart

Period # 13 SILENT PERIOD Sources: 1 & 2 Maccabees								
NEHEMIAH	Persian Rule	ALEXANDER	Greek Rule	DECREE	Indepen-dence	POMPEY	Roman Rule	CHRIST
400		332		142		63		6 BC

Review Time

We have now surveyed over 2,000 years of biblical history. Let's see what you have learned.

1. How long did the Beginnings and Scattering periods last?
2. Who came first...
   a. Abraham or Noah?
   b. Joshua or Gideon
   c. Hezekiah or Jezebel?
   d. Jeroboam or David?
   e. Deborah or Esther?
   f. Judas Maccabeus or Nehemiah
3. If you were reading these chapters, what period of biblical history would you be reading about?
   a. Joshua 1–24
   b. Numbers 1–36
   c. Exodus 1–15
   d. Genesis 46–50
   e. Genesis 12–45
   f. 1 Samuel 1–7
   g. 1 Kings 1–11
   h. Nehemiah 1–13
   i. 2 Kings 17–23

1. Uncertain.
2. a. Noah; b. Joshua; c. Jezebel; d. David; e. Deborah; f. Nehemiah.
3. a. Conquest; b. Wilderness; c. Egyptian; d. Egyptian; e. Pilgrim; f. Judges; g. Single Kingdom; h. Persian; i. Assyrian.

Silent Period

Chapter Fifteen

INCARNATION PERIOD
God in the Flesh

The term *incarnation* is taken from two Latin words *in caro, in flesh*. This is the technical word that Christians use to speak about how the eternal Son of God came in a human body to live among his people. You can read about the Incarnation Period of biblical history in the four Gospels—**Matthew, Mark, Luke,** and **John**. While there is much overlap in the information these writers convey, each presents Jesus from a different viewpoint.

Duration

The Incarnation Period began with events surrounding the birth of Christ. For reasons explained in the previous chapter, the birth announcements concerning John and Jesus probably came about 6 BC. A decree by the Roman Emperor Caesar Augustus forced Joseph and Mary to make a long trip to Bethlehem in order to register for taxation. The small village of Bethlehem was jam packed. There was no room for the couple in the local inn. Because Mary was near the time of giving birth, the innkeeper allowed the couple to occupy the stable, probably a cave beneath the inn. There Jesus was born. These events marked the beginning of the Incarnation Period of biblical history.

The Incarnation Period ended with the ascension of Jesus into heaven in AD 30. So the Incarnation Period lasted about **thirty-six years**.

Scriptural Theme

No single verse better captures the theme of the Incarnation Period than John 1:14. *"The Word became flesh and made his dwelling among us. We have seen his glory, the glory of the One and Only, who came from the Father, full of grace and truth."*

Key Players

The Incarnation Period is all about Jesus—his travels, his words, his claims, and his deeds. Everyone else functions in a supporting-cast role. Judging by frequency of mention, here are the seven individuals who rise to the level of major characters of this period. In addition to Jesus' herald (John the Baptist), there were three apostles and three antagonists.

- ❖ **Advance man:** John the Baptist
- ❖ **Apostles:** Peter, James, and John
- ❖ **Antagonists:** Herod, Pilate, and Judas

Advance man. **John** was important to the ministry of Jesus in the following ways. First, John, whose ministry preceded that of Jesus by a few months, prepared the Jewish people for the coming of Christ by preaching repentance and practicing baptism. Second, Jesus praised John as the greatest of the prophets (Matthew 11:11). Third, John baptized Jesus (Matthew 3:15). Fourth, Jesus' first disciples had also been disciples of John the Baptist (John 1:35-37). Fifth, John humbly directed his followers to Jesus. Some of them, however, refused to abandon John. According to the Jewish historian Josephus, Herod the Tetrarch executed John because "he feared that John's extensive influence over the people might lead to an uprising." John's movement did not stop with his death. Over two decades later Paul came across some disciples of John the Baptist in distant Ephesus (Acts 18:24-19:7).

Apostles. Jesus gave a disciple named *Simon* the name *Cephas* or **Peter**, which means *Rock*. He is called the son of John (John

1:42). In modern terms we might call him Peter Johnson. Peter came from the fishing village of Bethsaida (John 1:44). He was led to Christ by his less famous brother, Andrew. Both originally had been disciples of John the Baptist (John 1:35-42). Peter had a home in Capernaum, which virtually became Jesus' headquarters during his ministry in Galilee (Mark 1:21, 29). Clearly Peter was the leader among the twelve disciples whom Jesus called to fulltime ministry. As a member of Jesus' inner circle, Peter was privileged to witness some events that the other disciples did not see.

James and John were fishermen sons of Zebedee. They may have been Jesus' first cousins. The brothers probably lived in Capernaum from which they ran a commercial fishing enterprise on the Sea of Galilee. Along with Peter, James and John were also members of the "inner three" who were with Jesus on special occasions when the other disciples were not present. Apparently the two men were hotheads. They once wanted Jesus to call down fire to consume a village (Luke 9:54). Jesus nicknamed them *sons of thunder* (Mark 3:17). These brothers were also a bit presumptuous. They asked to sit in places of honor, on Jesus' left and right in his glory (Mark 10:35-41). This request earned the two a rebuke (Luke 22:8).

Antagonists. The first antagonist is one of several Herods mentioned in the New Testament. The one who was important during the Incarnation Period was **Herod the Tetrarch** (governor), or simply Herod T. He was the son of Herod the Great, the one who tried to kill baby Jesus. When Herod the Great died in 4 BC, Herod T was appointed to rule a portion of the kingdom previously ruled by his father. Like his father he was a great builder. One of his projects was the city of Tiberias on the Sea of Galilee, which still thrives to this day. John the Baptist was imprisoned and later beheaded by this king (Matthew 14:1-12). Jesus is recorded as having once described Herod T as *that fox* (Luke 13:31f). In the morning of the day of his crucifixion Jesus was questioned by Herod T (Luke 23:6-12).

The second antagonist was the *governor* (technical term *procurator*) of Judea during the closing years of Jesus' ministry. **Pontius**

Pilate appointed the Jewish high priests and controlled the Jerusalem temple. He outraged the Jews by misappropriating temple money to build an aqueduct to bring water into Jerusalem. Pilate was guilty of many atrocities against the Jewish people, including the one Jesus spoke about in Luke 13:1. Jesus stood trial twice before Pilate on the morning of his crucifixion. Because he was on thin ice with his superiors back in Rome, Pilate allowed himself to be pressured by Jewish religious authorities into ordering the crucifixion of Jesus. As an insult to the Jewish leadership he ordered this inscription put over Jesus' cross: *This is the King of the Jews*.

The third antagonist is the most famous of all. Of the seven men named Judas in the New Testament, the most famous by far is the disciple known as **Judas Iscariot**. He is always named last in lists of apostles because of his role as betrayer. Judas was the only one of Jesus' apostles who did not come from the region of Galilee. *Iscariot* means *man of Kerioth*, a town near Hebron in Judea. Judas acted as treasurer for the disciples; but he was known as a miser and a thief (John 12:5-6). He was present briefly at the Last Supper, during which Jesus predicted his betrayal (Matthew 26:20-21). Judas betrayed Jesus to the authorities for thirty pieces of silver. He led them to the garden late in the night. To identify Jesus in the darkness Judas kissed him on the cheek. Judas tried to return the silver to the priests. The Jewish leaders refused to take back their blood money. In despair Judas went out and hanged himself.

Major Events

The events of Jesus' ministry can be organized into seven periods:

- ❖ **Preparation (30 years)**
- ❖ **Year of Obscurity**
- ❖ **Year of Popularity**
- ❖ **Year of Opposition**

Incarnation Period

Incarnation Period

- ❖ **Persecution** (3 months)
- ❖ **Passion** (1 week)
- ❖ **Triumph** (40 days)

Preparation. Aside from the birth of Christ, which was part of the watershed event commencing this period, two other events stand out in the preparation phase of the life of Christ. The first is his *baptism*. When Jesus was about thirty (Luke 3:23), he traveled about seventy miles from Nazareth to where John was baptizing in the Jordan River. John did not want to baptize Jesus; but Jesus insisted that it was necessary in order to be pleasing to God. As Jesus emerged from the waters of his baptism, the Holy Spirit descended on him like a dove. A voice from heaven identified Jesus as God's Son. This unusual coming of the Spirit was a sign to John the Baptist that Jesus was the long awaited Messiah (John 1:33). Jesus' **baptism** marked the beginning of his public ministry. From this day forward John began to point his disciples to Jesus.

The second event of importance in the preparation period was the **wilderness temptations**. From his baptism Jesus went immediately into the wilderness area near the river. There he fasted and prayed. The devil tempted him during that time (Matthew 4:1; Luke 4:2). Three of those temptations are recorded. In each case Jesus answered the temptation with a quotation from Scripture. He refused to use his miraculous powers for personal advantage, to engage in some spectacular stunt, or to take any shortcut to establishing his kingdom. The wilderness temptations were a time of testing for Jesus. He passed the test!

Year of Obscurity. During the first year of Jesus' ministry he was not widely known. He quietly taught and built a core group of followers. Jesus' **first miracle**, however, makes our list of the twelve most important events in Jesus' life. This miracle was performed in the village of Cana of Galilee not far from his hometown of Nazareth (John 2:1-11). He and some of the earliest disciples attended a wedding feast at which his mother Mary was a hostess. During the course of the celebration the wine ran out. Mary informed Jesus of the situation, hinting that he should help. Jesus was reluctant to use his power for such a private matter. Nonetheless, Jesus told servants to fill six large jars to the brim with water. Then they were to take some of that water to the man in charge. When this man tasted the water it had turned into the best wine that had yet been served at the banquet. The people attending the festivities did not know the origin of the wine; but Jesus' disciples did. From this time on they began to put their faith in Jesus.

Year of Popularity. In the second year of his ministry Jesus was very popular with the masses of people, especially in the Galilee region. The climax of his popularity was the **feeding of the 5,000**. A large crowd had followed Jesus into a remote area. There was no place for them to purchase food. A survey indicated that among the entire crowd only one boy had any food with him. He had five small pancakes of bread and two small fish. Jesus said a prayer over the bread and fish. The disciples began to distribute it to the people. The food was multiplied so that all were filled. Several baskets of leftovers were taken up. The crowds wanted to proclaim Jesus as king on the spot (Matthew 14:13-21). Shortly after this great miracle Jesus preached a sermon in which he said he had not come to provide free lunches. He came to bring spiritual bread (John 6:25-59). Many of the Jews quit following Jesus because of this sermon.

Year of Opposition. The third full year of Jesus' ministry was marked by rising opposition from the religious leaders. Jesus was forced to withdraw to regions inhabited by Gentiles and less zealous Jews. The first event during this period to make our list of top twelve was **Peter's confession.** Jesus had taken his disciples to the region of Caesarea Philippi north of Galilee. His popularity with the masses was at its lowest point. Jesus asked his disciples who the people thought he was. Some thought he was John the Baptist, or Elijah, Jeremiah, or one of the Old Testament prophets. Then Jesus asked who the disciples thought he was. Peter, speaking for the rest, said, *"You are the Christ, the Son of the living God"* (Matthew 16:16). Peter's confession became foundational for Christian faith.

Incarnation Period

The second important event of this period, the **transfiguration**, occurred a week after Peter's great confession. Jesus took his inner circle (Peter, James, John) up into a high mountain. We think this may have been Mount Hermon, the highest mountain in the region. For a few moments Jesus' body glowed with heavenly glory. Moses and Elijah appeared to converse with Jesus about his coming death (Matthew 17).

Persecution. During the last three months of his ministry Jesus was hounded by his enemies. While ministering across the Jordan River in a region called Perea, Jesus received news that his good friend Lazarus was near death. Jesus deliberately delayed two more days during which time Lazarus died. Jesus then took his disciples to Bethany where the deceased man had lived. He asked to be taken to the cave where Lazarus was buried. Jesus called forth Lazarus from the dead. The **resurrection of Lazarus** must be considered the greatest of Jesus' miracles. It was performed only two miles or so from Jerusalem, the center of opposition to Jesus. After this miracle the religious leaders determined to kill Jesus, and Lazarus too (John 11).

Passion Week. The last week of Jesus' ministry is called the Passion Week because of the suffering that Jesus experienced. Two events during that eventful week make our list of the most important events in the life of Christ. On the first day of this week Jesus made his **triumphal entry** into Jerusalem. He came riding on the back of a small donkey, just as the prophet Zechariah had foretold. Supporters from Galilee waved palm branches and hailed him as their king. This further enraged the Jerusalem religious leaders. In the triumphal entry Jesus was making a public declaration that he was the Messiah of prophecy and the long-anticipated Savior (Matthew 21).

The second event of Passion Week to make our list of the twelve most significant events was the **crucifixion**, which took place on Friday. In crucifixion a victim was nailed to a cross. He was hung in a position that made breathing very difficult. Jesus was on the cross for six hours. Only five of his disciples are named as having been there to give him encouragement. To humiliate him, Jesus was executed naked between two notorious criminals. He spoke seven famous sayings from the cross. By 3:00 PM he was dead. A soldier thrust a spear through his side just to make sure. No one, not even his closest disciples, understood the full significance of the cross until after the resurrection.

Triumph. The forty days of triumph began three days after Jesus was buried. In this phase there are two important events to make the list of twelve. The first event was Jesus' **resurrection** from the dead. Jesus was hastily buried on Friday afternoon just before the start of the Sabbath when no work could be done by the Jews. Some of Jesus' female disciples intended to return Sunday morning to complete the burial preparations. When they got to the tomb it was empty. Angels announced that Jesus was alive (Matthew 28). Then Jesus began appearing to various disciples around Jerusalem. By that night the disciples were convinced that Jesus had conquered death (Luke 24). Not being present in the room when Jesus appeared, Thomas doubted. Jesus appeared to the eleven disciples. He invited Thomas to touch the wounds in his body (John 20). Thereafter Jesus appeared to his disciples in Galilee, including one occasion when he met with a group of about five hundred (1 Corinthians 15:6). Belief in the resurrection of Jesus is the cornerstone of the Christian faith.

For the last of the twelve greatest events in the life of Christ see under Watershed Event.

Great Miracles

Of the many miracles Jesus performed, thirty-six are described in the four Gospels. Only two of those are recorded in all four Gospels—the feeding of the 5,000, and the restoring of a severed ear. Jesus' first and last miracles were recorded only by John—the first being the turning water into wine (John 2:7-9), the last being a large catch of fish (John 21:6). Matthew contains the largest number of miracles (22); but John has the most miracles not recorded in one of the other three Gospels (6).

The miracles of Jesus break down into four categories: healing miracles (17), rebuking miracles (7), and resurrection miracles (3) — the young girl, the widow's son, and Lazarus. Jesus also performed nine nature miracles.

God's Message

The greatest revelation of all of biblical history took place when Christ entered the world to reveal to us the Father. Jesus once said, *"Anyone who has seen me has seen the Father"* (John 14:9). On another occasion he said: *"I and the Father are one"* (John 10:30). In addition, the teachings of Christ also reveal much to us about the nature of God and his will for our lives. In this simple overview of biblical history we only have space to highlight three aspects of Jesus' teaching.

First, the **most important public sermon** Jesus delivered was the Sermon on the Mount (Matthew 5-7). In this sermon Jesus touched on such subjects as discipleship, authority, prayer, and wise choices.

Second, **the most important private teaching** of Jesus was delivered on the night of his betrayal when he spoke to his disciples about the coming of the Holy Spirit into the world (John 14-16).

Third, **the most prominent form** of Jesus' teaching was the parable. A parable is a comparison of a spiritual truth with an everyday experience. Jesus especially used parables to illustrate life in his spiritual kingdom. Not all his parables are clearly labeled. This makes it hard to give the precise number recorded in the Gospels. Can you name some of Jesus' parables?

Old Testament Anticipation

Scholars have found at least seventy-two passages in the Old Testament that anticipate the Incarnation Period. The entire life of

Jesus was outlined prophetically before he came into this world. Here are a few of the key Old Testament predictions:

- ❖ **His virgin birth** (Isaiah 7:14)
- ❖ **His birth place** (Micah 5:2)
- ❖ **His commencement of ministry** (Daniel 9:25)
- ❖ **His deity** (Psalms 2:7; 45:6; 110:1; Isaiah 9:6)
- ❖ **His crucifixion** (Psalm 22; Isaiah 53)
- ❖ **His resurrection** (Isaiah 53:10)

Watershed Event

The Incarnation Period ended with the **ascension** of Jesus into heaven forty days after his resurrection. After some weeks, the disciples returned to Jerusalem. There Jesus met with them one last time. He told them to wait in Jerusalem where they would receive special power from heaven. Then he walked with them to the Mount of Olives near Bethany. There they saw him slowly ascend into heaven. Two angels appeared to assure them that the same Jesus they had seen go into heaven will one day return in like manner (Acts 1). So the Incarnation Period starts in a manger and ends on the Mount of Olives; it begins in Bethlehem and ends near Bethany (Luke 24:50).

Incarnation Period

Summary Chart

Period # 14 INCARNATION PERIOD Matthew, Mark, Luke, & John					
B I R T H Events	Preparation 30 Years	Ministry* 3½ Years	Triumph 40 Days	A S C E N D S	
6 BC	6 BC–AD 26	AD 26–30	AD 30	AD 30	
*For details see under Major Events above.					

Review Time

1. Can you name the ten periods of the Mosaic Age?
2. In what period did the following take place:
   a. Noah built an altar.
   b. Abraham "sacrificed" his son
   c. Eve ate forbidden fruit
   d. Samson slew 1,000 Philistines
   e. Solomon built the Temple
   f. Nehemiah built the wall
   g. Translation of Old Testament into Greek
   h. Nebuchadnezzar destroys Jerusalem
   i. Esther saves her people from genocide
   j. Joshua conquers the Promised Land
   k. Ten plagues on Egypt.
3. What pivotal character was active . . .
   a. about 2000 BC?
   b. about 1400 BC?
   c. about 1000 BC?
   d. about 400 BC?
4. Watershed event between . . .
   a. Beginnings and Scattering periods?
   b. Silent and Incarnation periods?
   c. Assyrian and Babylonian periods?
   d. Judges and Single Kingdom periods?
   e. Egyptian and Wilderness periods?

1. Wilderness; Conquest; Judges; Single Kingdom; Sister Kingdoms; Assyrian; Babylonian; Persian; Silent; Incarnation.
2. a. Scattering; b. Pilgrim; c. Beginnings; d. Judges; e. Single Kingdom; f. Persian; g. Silent; h. Babylonian; i. Persian; j. Conquest; k. Egyptian.
3. a. Abraham; b. Moses; c. David; d. Nehemiah.
4. a. Flood; b. birth announcements; c. Carchemish battle; d. anointing of Saul; e. Exodus or Crossing of Red Sea.

Incarnation Period

Chapter Sixteen

POURING PERIOD
To the Jew First

The decade following the ascension of Christ is clearly a distinct period in New Testament history, but it is difficult to give a name to it. It could be called the Petrine Period, after Peter. He was the leading figure in this period. That name, however, tends to overlook the contribution of all the others. It could be called the Birthday Period, for during this decade the church of Christ was born. It could be called the Proclamation Period, or the Great Commission Period, but these names do not distinguish this decade from those that followed.

The term *outpouring* refers to the coming of the Holy Spirit in power. This miraculous outpouring occurred at the beginning, in the middle and at the end of this period. The Pouring Period is documented in **Acts 1–11.** (Acts is the fifth book of the New Testament).

Duration

A brief ten-day interim followed the close of the Incarnation Period. During those ten days the disciples of Jesus in the Jerusalem area gathered to pray. Peter led a Bible study that guided them to select a replacement for Judas the betrayer. (Judas had committed suicide when he saw that he could not "undo" his betrayal of the Lord.) Only those who had been disciples of Jesus since the beginning of his ministry were eligible. Two men qualified. The group prayed that God would make clear his choice between the two men. Then the disciples cast lots, a process like the modern "drawing straws." Thereafter Mathias became the twelfth apostle of Jesus (Acts 1).

Pentecost (*pehn´-tih-kawst*) was a major Jewish feast day. Jews from all over the world had come to Jerusalem for Passover fifty days earlier. Most of them remained in the city to participate in the Pentecost feast. The disciples of Jesus were occupying a chamber off the temple courts as the Pentecost festivities began. The people in the temple courts heard a sound like a tornado. Shafts of light suddenly appeared that looked like tongues of fire. These tongues of fire hovered momentarily over the heads of the apostles. The sound and sight brought thousands near to where the apostles were residing. The Twelve began to speak the praise of God in the native languages of the people who had gathered. Peter took the opportunity to preach the first gospel sermon of the Christian Age. Three thousand accepted the claims of Christ that day. They demonstrated their faith by being baptized. So on that Pentecost morning, in Jerusalem, in AD 30 the church of Christ was born.

The Pouring Period lasted from Pentecost until the outpouring of God's Spirit on the house of Cornelius the Gentile. We cannot compute exactly how much time elapsed between these two events. New Testament scholars estimate that it was from eight to ten years. So for the purposes of this simplified version of biblical history, we will say that the Pouring Period lasted AD **30–39**, or **ten years**.

Scriptural Theme

"God has raised this Jesus to life, and we are all witnesses of the fact. Exalted to the right hand of God, he has received from the Father the promised Holy Spirit and has poured out what you now see and hear" (Acts 2:32-33). These words of Peter explained to the Pentecost crowd the unusual sights and sounds that they had witnessed that day in the temple courts.

Pouring Period

Pouring Period

Key Players

There are eight major characters in the Pouring Period. They break down into three groups:

- ❖ **Two apostles**
- ❖ **Two deacons**
- ❖ **Four converts**

Apostles. Without question Simon **Peter** was the leader during the first decade of Christianity. He arranged for the selection of an apostle to replace Judas (Acts 1). Peter preached the first and last recorded sermons in this period (Acts 2, 10). He was involved in healing two lame men and raising a woman (Dorcas) from the dead (Acts 3, 9). Peter also baptized the first Gentile convert (Acts 10). The second key player of this period was the Apostle **John**. He was Peter's coworker during the early years of the Pouring Period. He was with Peter when a lame man was healed at the temple gate (Acts 3). John and Peter were arrested by the temple authorities. Shortly thereafter all the apostles were arrested and flogged. They were warned not to preach any further in the name of Jesus. Peter and John were instrumental in passing on to the new Samaritan Christian leaders the special gift of the Holy Spirit (Acts 8:14-17).

Deacons. Seven men were selected by the Jerusalem congregation to distribute food to needy widows. Two of these men became prominent. After receiving the laying on of the apostles' hands **Stephen** (*stih´-fehn*) was able to perform great wonders and miraculous signs among the people (Acts 6:8). Stephen was the first Christian, other than an apostle, who is known to have performed such miracles. He entered into the synagogues of the Greek-speaking Jews in Jerusalem and argued persuasively with them that Jesus was the Christ. Not being able to refute Stephen in public debate, the Jews took him before the Sanhedrin, the highest court in Judaism. They misrepresented what Stephen had preached. The Sanhedrin gave Stephen the opportunity to speak in his own defense. His marvelous sermon, recorded in Acts 7, so enraged the Jewish audience that they stoned Stephen to death. He was the first Christian who is known to have become a martyr for the faith.

The second of the Jerusalem deacons to make our list of key players was **Philip** (*fihl´-ihp*). Philip the deacon/evangelist is not to be confused with Philip the Apostle, one of the Twelve. When Philip left Jerusalem because of persecution, he chose to make the region of Samaria his mission field. Philip overcame prejudice against the Samaritans that he had been taught from his youth. He was the first to carry the gospel to these people who were so despised by the Jews. Many of the Samaritans obeyed the gospel. An angel called Philip away from that successful effort to minister to a man traveling back to Ethiopia (Acts 8). After baptizing that man into Christ, Philip preached in the coastal cities of Palestine establishing many congregations of believers.

Converts. Four converts make our list of key players in the Pouring Period. The first was **Simon the Sorcerer.** In Samaria Philip was able to bring a notable deceiver to Christ. After being baptized Simon followed Philip around astonished by the great miracles Philip was performing. Simon observed that through the laying on of the hands of the apostles certain Samaritan converts were given special gifts of the Spirit. Simon tried to purchase from the apostles this power so that he too could give special gifts by the laying on of his hands. Peter was horrified at the thought. He rebuked Simon in the strongest words. Shocked by the rebuke, Simon requested prayer for himself (Acts 8).

Another key player in this period was an unnamed **Ethiopian.** An angel sent Philip to a lonely desert road where a Jew from Ethiopia was traveling home from one of the Jewish festivals. Philip got up into his chariot with him. He explained the prophecy of Isaiah 53 to the man. He told him about Jesus. As they continued along the road they came to a pool of water. The Ethiopian asked Philip to baptize him (Acts 8). This African returned to his homeland to share the gospel and establish the church on the continent of Africa.

The third convert to make the key player list is **Saul of Tarsus** (*tahr´-suhs*). Saul was a brilliant rabbinical student and one of the leaders in the Jewish persecution of the Christians. Eventually Saul changed his name to Paul. He became the greatest theologian and defender of Christianity in the early years. See further below under Major Events.

The fourth convert to make the key player list is **Cornelius** (*kor-nee´-lee-uhs*). He was a Roman soldier stationed in Caesarea (*say-sahr-ree´-uh*), the Roman capital of the region. This man had been exposed to the teachings of the Old Testament through his contacts with the Jews. He was a believer in God. He prayed daily. He did what he could to help the poor. Cornelius, however, needed to know Christ. God sent an angel to tell this soldier to send for Peter who was in the general area. When he heard Peter preach the gospel, Cornelius became the first Gentile convert to Christianity.

Major Events

The outpourings of the Spirit at the beginning and end of the Pouring Period were certainly major. Between those two outpourings, however, were five incidents that rise to the level of major events.

- ❖ **Temple healing**
- ❖ **Hypocrites died**
- ❖ **Deacons ordained**
- ❖ **Stephen stoned**
- ❖ **Saul converted**

Temple healing (Acts 3). Of the many miracles being performed by the apostles during those earliest days of the church, only the temple healing of a lame man is recorded in detail (Acts 3). The reason this particular miracle is highlighted is because of the ramifications it had for the church. This miracle was performed in the temple precincts, an area controlled by the priests who were Sadducees. It set the stage for the second recorded gospel sermon. Like the first gospel sermon, this one also was preached by Peter. The sermon focused on Jesus and his resurrection. Peter's sermon was interrupted by the temple police, who were controlled by the priests. They were not going to permit any preaching about Jesus on their turf! Peter and John were arrested and put in jail overnight. The next day they were warned by the Sanhedrin (Jewish court) not to preach in the name of Jesus. So the healing of the lame man at the temple gate led to the first official religious opposition to the growing church.

Death of hypocrites *(Acts 5)*. Ananias *(an-uh-ni´-uhs)* and his wife Sapphira *(suhp-fi´-ruh)* sold some property. They agreed that they would present a portion of the proceeds to the church. They pretended, however, that they were giving the entire amount to the Lord. It seems that they wanted the praise of the other Christians. So one at a time—first Ananias, then later his wife—they came before the apostles and told their lie. Both the husband and his wife died on the spot. *"Great fear seized the whole church and all who heard about these events"* (Acts 5:11). At the outset of Christianity God was warning his people that he deals most harshly with hypocrites. The result was that those who were not sincere in their faith avoided the Christians. On the other hand, those who truly loved the Lord accepted Christ and were added to the church (Acts 5:13-14).

Deacons ordained *(Acts 6)*. The Greek-speaking members of the church began to grumble because they perceived that their widows were not being given the same amount each day as the Aramaic-speaking widows. The Twelve proposed that seven men be elected to assume the responsibility for the daily distribution. The congregation selected the men—all with Greek names. These men were then ordained by the apostles for this important ministry. They are not called *deacons* in the text. Many, however, feel that this incident at least set the precedent for having deacons in local congregations. The incident with the seven deacons is signif-

Pouring Period

icant for several reasons. First, it solved an internal problem within the church in a constructive way. Second, it set a precedent about how a local church comes to have leaders. Third, when the apostles laid their hands on these seven, they conferred upon them the power to perform miracles in the name of Jesus. Two of these seven are the first Christians other than apostles to perform miracles (Acts 6:8; 8:6).

Stephen stoned *(Acts 7)*. The stoning of Stephen marked an escalation in the persecution against Christians in Jerusalem. His death led to a scattering of the Christians in all directions (Acts 8:1).

Saul converted *(Acts 9)*. Saul was the leading opponent of Christianity in the early years. He encountered Christ while on a mission to arrest Christians in Damascus. As he was approaching Damascus, Saul saw a blinding light. He heard Jesus speak to him from heaven. The Lord directed Saul to proceed on to Damascus. There a local preacher came to restore Saul's sight and baptize him into Christ. Saul immediately began to preach the gospel in the synagogues of Damascus. Sometime later Saul teamed up in a teaching ministry with Barnabas in the fast-growing church in Antioch *(an´-tih-ahkh)*. It was during that time that the disciples began to be called *Christians* (Acts 11:26). The conversion of Saul brought an end to the religious persecution of the Christians by the Jewish authorities in Jerusalem.

Great Miracles

The miraculous speaking in unlearned languages was a sign that the Holy Spirit had been poured out on Pentecost and ten years later in the house of Cornelius (Acts 2:4; 10:46). Something like that must also have occurred when Peter and John laid their hands on the new Samaritan Christians (Acts 8:18). During the earliest days of Christianity the apostles were performing wonders and signs almost on a daily basis (Acts 2:43; 5:12-16). After receiving the laying on of the apostles' hands, Stephen and Philip also performed wonders and signs (Acts 6:8; 8:6, 13). The great miracles of the Pouring Period are these:

- ❖ Temple healing
- ❖ Prison escape
- ❖ Paralytic healed
- ❖ Dorcas raised

Temple healing (Acts 3). A man crippled from birth was carried to one of the temple gates every day. There he begged from those entering or leaving the temple. One day Peter and John stopped in front of this man. They asked him to look at them. Then they commanded him in the name of Jesus to walk. Peter helped the man to his feet. Instantly the man's feet and ankles became strong. He jumped to his feet and began walking and leaping and praising God. The ramifications of this miracle were spelled out above in the Major Events section.

Prison escape (Acts 5:19). The apostles were arrested by the temple authorities. They were put into the public jail. During the night an angel of the Lord opened the doors of the jail and brought them out. The angel told the apostles to return to the temple and preach the gospel. This they did. They were rearrested the following day and flogged by the temple officials.

Paralytic healed (Acts 9:32-35). While visiting the new Christians living in the coastal pains of Palestine, Peter encountered Aeneas (*aye-nee´-uhs*). He had been bedridden with paralysis for eight years. Peter announced the man's healing. He commanded him to arise from his bed. The miracle jump-started the growth of the church in the outlying region of Judea.

Dorcas raised (Acts 9:36-41). Shortly after the healing of Aeneas, a prominent Christian woman in nearby Joppa died. Her body was washed according to the custom of the time. It was laid in an upstairs room awaiting burial. The Christians summoned Peter. When the apostle entered the room he was surrounded by weeping widows. They displayed the garments that Dorcas (*door´-kuhs*) had made for the poor. Peter put the mourners out of the room. He got down on his knees and prayed by the bedside.

Pouring Period

Normally apostles did not pray when performing healing miracles. This, however, was different. The woman was already dead. Peter needed to clear the matter with the Boss first before attempting to raise Dorcas from the dead. He then took the woman by the hand. He told her to get up. Dorcas opened her eyes and sat up. Peter then helped Dorcas to her feet. He presented her alive to her fellow believers. This miracle had a tremendous impact on the coastal area. Many turned to the Lord.

God's Message

The apostles were guided by the Holy Spirit into all truth. For this reason the Pouring Period is full of revelation. Four revelations, however, rise to the level of most important.

- ❖ **Christ enthroned**
- ❖ **Forgiveness offered**
- ❖ **Barriers removed**
- ❖ **Herald appointed**

Christ enthroned. In the first gospel sermon Peter revealed to his audience the fact that Christ had ascended into heaven after his resurrection. Peter pointed to the sights and sounds of Pentecost and the miraculous speaking in unlearned languages as proof that Christ had poured out the Holy Spirit from his heavenly throne. In addition, he cited Old Testament prophecies that predicted this enthronement (Acts 2:31-35). Pentecost marked the beginning of the reign of Christ, the heavenly kingdom of which John the Baptist and Jesus had spoken so frequently during the Incarnation Period.

Forgiveness offered. The Jews who heard Peter preach on Pentecost were cut to the heart by his words. They now realized that they had committed a terrible sin by rejecting Jesus and demanding his execution. The Jews cried out in desperation, *"What shall we do?"* The asking of this question implied that these

Jews now acknowledged Christ—they believed in him. Peter told these sinners to *"repent and be baptized, every one of you, in the name of Jesus Christ for the forgiveness of your sins. And you will receive the gift of the Holy Spirit"* (Acts 2:38). Under the reign of Christ sinners need to believe in Christ, repent of their sin, and be baptized for the forgiveness of their sins. Only when they have accepted the gospel on these terms can they have biblical assurance of their forgiveness and salvation.

Barriers removed. Jesus commissioned his followers to go into the world and preach the gospel to every creature. For almost ten years the church did not reach out to Gentiles. While he was praying on top of the flat roof of the house where he was staying, Peter fell into a trance. He saw a sheet with clean and unclean animals lowered from heaven. He was told to eat from the unclean meat. Being of Jewish background Peter was horrified at the thought. Three times the sheet was lowered. Three times the voice directed Peter to eat. At first Peter puzzled over the meaning of his vision. Then messengers arrived from the Gentile Cornelius inviting Peter to come and preach the good news. Peter now understood that God was signaling that all barriers separating Jews and Gentiles had been removed. Gentiles were not to be considered unclean and off limits to the gospel of Christ (Acts 10).

Herald appointed. The Lord revealed to a preacher named Ananias (same name as the earlier hypocrite) the future ministry of Saul of Tarsus. Saul was God's chosen instrument to carry Christ's name to the Gentiles (Acts 9:15).

Old Testament Anticipation

Peter explained to the Pentecost crowd that what they were witnessing was the fulfillment of a prediction made by the prophet Joel 850 years before Christ. *"No, this is what was spoken by the prophet Joel: In the last days, God says, I will pour out my Spirit on all people"* (Acts 2:16-17). Pentecost marked the beginning of the Age of the Spirit anticipated by Joel.

Pouring Period

Watershed Event

As Peter preached the gospel to those gathered in the house of Cornelius, his sermon was interrupted. God poured out on Cornelius the Holy Spirit from heaven just like he had poured out on the apostles on the day of Pentecost ten years earlier. Peter knew for sure that God was signaling his acceptance of Gentiles. Peter ordered the immediate baptism of those present in the house.

Peter was the focus of criticism from Jewish Christians when he baptized the first Gentile converts. When Peter was explaining what happened at the house of Cornelius, he made this comment:

> *As I began to speak, the Holy Spirit came on them as he had come on us at the beginning. Then I remembered what the Lord had said: "John baptized with water, but you will be baptized with the Holy Spirit." So if God gave them the same gift as he gave us, who believed in the Lord Jesus Christ, who was I to think that I could oppose God?* (Acts 11:15-17).

These words of Peter link what happened at the house of Cornelius with what happened on the day of Pentecost in Acts 2. They also link both events to John's promise of a baptism with the Holy Spirit (Matthew 3:11). The two outpourings or baptisms of the Holy Spirit are the watershed events marking the beginning and end of the Pouring Period.

Summary Chart

	Period # 15 POURING PERIOD Acts 1–11					
P O U R I N G	Church Stationary in Jerusalem Area			Church Scattered to Antioch Area		P O U R I N G
			Stephen's Death			
Pentecost	Lame Man Healed	Deacons Selected	Samaria Campaign		Saul Converted	Cornelius
AD 30	AD 30–34		AD 34–39			AD 39
Acts 1–2	Acts 3–6		Acts 7–9			Acts 10–11

Pouring Period

Chapter Seventeen

PAULINE PERIOD
To the Ends of the Earth

Saul—later called Paul—had two notable ministries prior to being sent out to serve as a missionary. Immediately after his baptism he preached Christ in the synagogues of Damascus (*duh-mass´-kuhs*) (Acts 9:20-22). He then made a brief trip to Jerusalem. From there he returned to his hometown of Tarsus. The record is silent about what he did in the way of preaching while there. About the year AD 41 Barnabas brought Saul to work with him in the growing church at Antioch (Acts 11:25-26).

About the year AD 45 the Holy Spirit called Saul (Paul) and Barnabas to go forth as missionaries. After this Paul became the key figure in the advancement of Christianity, especially among the Gentiles.

Most of the Pauline Period is documented in **Acts 12–28**. In addition, some details of Paul's life can be reconstructed from references in the epistles that Paul wrote.

Duration

The Pauline Period may be said to date from the conversion of Cornelius (about AD 39), although Paul did not become a prominent church figure until about six years later. The Pauline Period ends with the confinement of Paul in Rome about AD 63. So the Pauline Period lasted about **24 years**.

Scriptural Theme

The essence of the Pauline Period and the spirit of Paul himself are captured in these words that the great apostle penned:

> *I will not venture to speak of anything except what Christ has accomplished through me in leading the Gentiles to obey God by what I have said and done – by the power of signs and miracles, through the power of the Spirit. So from Jerusalem all the way around to Illyricum [modern Albania], I have fully proclaimed the gospel of Christ. It has always been my ambition to preach the gospel where Christ was not known, so that I would not be building on someone else's foundation* (Romans 15:18-20).

Key Players

Obviously Paul is the major character of the Pauline Period. Others who figure prominently in the Pauline Period can be divided into two categories:

Paul's Associates	**Other Leaders**
❖ Barnabas	❖ Peter
❖ Silas	❖ James
❖ Timothy	(Jesus' brother)
❖ Titus	❖ Apollos
❖ Aquila & Priscilla	(the Evangelist)

Paul's associates. The earliest of Paul's associates in ministry was **Barnabas** (*bahr´-nuh-buhs*). He had been a coteacher with Paul in Antioch. On one occasion Barnabas wavered on the issue of full acceptance of Gentile Christians (Galatians 2:13). He traveled with Paul on what is called the first missionary journey. Barnabas was one of the main speakers at the Jerusalem conference when the status of converted Gentiles was discussed (Acts 15). Thereafter he had a disagreement with Paul over whether or not to take John Mark with them on the second missionary journey. The two missionaries decided to go their separate ways. Barnabas returned to Cyprus to encourage the new Christians there.

The second of Paul's key associates was **Silas** (*si´-luhs*), also called Silvanus (*sihl-vay´-nuhs*). He first surfaced after the Jerusalem conference in AD 50. Silas was commissioned to carry news of the Jerusalem conference to the believers at Antioch (Acts 15:22). He later became Paul's companion on the second missionary journey. He and Paul were beaten in Philippi. They spent a night in the city jail. Silas is mentioned along with Paul and Timothy in the opening verses of both of the letters to the Thessalonians. Following Paul's second missionary journey Silas teamed with Peter on missions in Pontus (*pahn´-tuhs*) and Cappadocia (*kap-puh-doh´-see-uh*), Roman provinces in what is today Turkey. Silas also served as Peter's scribe, penning the words of 1 Peter (1 Peter 5:12).

Paul asked the young man **Timothy** to accompany him on the second missionary journey. Timothy first heard the gospel when Paul passed through Lystra (*lihs´-truh*) on the first missionary journey. Paul sent Timothy on many crucial missions (Acts 17:14-15; 18:5; 19:22; 20:4; Romans 16:21; 1 Corinthians 16:10; 2 Corinthians 1:19; 1 Thessalonians 3:2, 6). For example, when he was unable to go to Corinth (*koh´-rinth*), Paul sent Timothy to represent him and his teachings (1 Corinthians 4:17). Timothy is mentioned along with Paul in the opening verses of six New Testament letters. In addition Paul sent two letters to Timothy to encourage and instruct him in his ministry. The last letter Paul ever wrote was to Timothy.

Another key associate of Paul's is for some strange reason not mentioned in the Book of Acts. It is clear from Paul's letters, however, that **Titus** (*tie´-tuhs*) was one of the apostle's right-hand men. He was entrusted with the delicate task of delivering Paul's severe letter (2 Corinthians 2:1-4) to Corinth and correcting problems within the church there (2 Corinthians 7:13-15). Successful in this mission Titus reported in person to Paul who was anxiously awaiting word in Macedonia (2 Corinthians 2:13; 7:5-6, 13-15). Paul responded by writing 2 Corinthians which Titus probably delivered (2 Corinthians 8:6, 16-18, 23).

Among the key associates of Paul were **Aquila and Priscilla**, a married couple the apostle originally met in Corinth. They were tentmakers like Paul (2 Timothy 4:19; Acts 18:2). This committed duo was left by Paul in Ephesus at the end of his second missionary journey (Acts 18:19) to prepare the field for the future endeavors. A church met in their home. They joined Paul in writing to the Corinthian church from Ephesus (1 Corinthians 16:19). A reference in Romans (16:3) probably indicates that Priscilla and Aquila (*ak´-wil-ah*) were in Rome. The couple risked their lives for Paul (Romans 16:4). In the last reference to the couple they are back in Ephesus assisting Timothy (2 Timothy 4:19).

Other leaders. Besides those who worked directly with Paul, three other Christian leaders make our list of key players in the Pauline Period. **Peter** continued his leadership role in the church during the Pauline Period. King Herod arrested Peter and intended to execute him. An angel of God opened the prison gates. Peter escaped. After Herod's death Peter returned to Jerusalem. He was one of the major speakers at the Jerusalem conference where the status of Gentiles in the church was discussed (Acts 15).

During the Pauline Period, **James the brother of Jesus** rose to prominence in the Jerusalem congregation. He spoke at the Jerusalem conference concerning the status of Gentiles in the church (Acts 15). James saw his calling as being to the Jews (Galatians 2:9). During this period James wrote a book of our New Testament. Some scholars think it was the first book of the New Testament to be written.

The third leader not associated with Paul was **Apollos the Evangelist** who came from Alexandria, Egypt. He was a disciple of John the Baptist. While visiting Ephesus he met Paul's friends Aquila and Priscilla. They showed him the way of the Lord more perfectly (Acts 18:24-26). Though he was learned in Scripture and a powerful speaker, he was not too proud to learn from the tent-

Pauline Period

maker couple. Apollos became a forceful advocate of the Christian faith. Paul considered him to be a faithful minister of the gospel (1 Corinthians 16:12). The last mention of Apollos (*ay-pahl´-lahs*) is in Titus 3:13 where Paul asked Titus to help Apollos on his way.

Major Events

Seven events were of major importance during the Pauline Period. These are:

- ❖ **Execution of Apostle James**
- ❖ **First Missionary Journey**
- ❖ **Jerusalem Conference**
- ❖ **Second Missionary Journey**
- ❖ **Third Missionary Journey**
- ❖ **Paul's Caesarea Imprisonment**
- ❖ **Journey to Rome**

Execution of James (Acts 12). King Herod (grandson of Herod the Great) tried to curry favor with the Jews in Jerusalem by arresting and *executing James* the Apostle. He was killed with the sword. James was the first of the Twelve to die for his faith.

First missionary journey (Acts 13–14). Paul's first missionary journey can be dated to the years AD 45–48. Barnabas was Paul's companion on this trip. John Mark, author of the Gospel of Mark, started out with the missionaries, but turned back early on. Paul visited the island of Cyprus where a Roman official was converted. Then the missionaries traveled through the Roman provinces that today would be in the country of Turkey. In the city of Antioch (a different Antioch from the one that dispatched the missionaries) Paul preached his first recorded sermon. Churches were established in the cities of Antioch, Iconium (*i-koh´-nih-um*), Lystra and Derbe (*dehr´- bih*). After establishing a church in Derbe, the missionaries turned around and retraced their steps. They appointed elders in every city. Then the missionaries sailed back to their home base in Syria. The first missionary journey covered over 1200 miles.

Jerusalem conference (Acts 15). False teachers went out from Jerusalem claiming to have the backing of the apostles. They were telling Gentiles that they needed to obey the Law of Moses or they could not be Christians. Paul and Barnabas stood up to these teachers. They went to Jerusalem to discuss with the apostles and elders the status of Gentiles in the church. It turned out that the teachers did not have the backing of the apostles. Peter, Paul, Barnabas, and James the Lord's brother spoke at the conference. The leaders set forth the position of the church regarding Gentiles in an open letter to the churches. The letter stated that Gentiles were not required to be circumcised or obey the Mosaic Law.

Second missionary journey (Acts 16–18). The second missionary journey is dated AD 51–53. Silas, Timothy, and Luke, the author of the Book of Acts, accompanied Paul on this journey. The journey started out by land through the region of modern Turkey. When the missionaries reached the Aegean Sea, Paul had a vision that summoned him to cross over to the continent of Europe to preach. That he did. Lydia, a merchant woman, became the first European convert to Christianity. The missionaries established churches in the cities of Philippi, Thessalonica (*thehs-suh-loh-ni´-kuh*), Berea, and Corinth, all in the area that we call today Greece. The team sailed home from Corinth. On this trip Paul wrote the New Testament books of 1 & 2 Thessalonians. This journey covered over 2300 miles.

Third missionary journey (Acts 19–20). After a brief rest in his home base of Antioch, Paul set out on the third missionary journey (AD 54–57). Outward bound there is no record of his traveling companions (if any). Homeward bound he was accompanied by seven representatives of the churches. They were carrying an offering for the poor Christians in Jerusalem. The great city of Ephesus (*ehf´-uh-sus*) on the coast of modern day Turkey was Paul's headquarters during this journey. Paul did, however, make

Pauline Period

a quick trip through Greece to deal with issues in the churches there. During the third missionary journey Paul wrote four books of the New Testament: Romans, Galatians, 1 & 2 Corinthians. On this journey Paul covered about the same distance as he did on his second journey.

Caesarea imprisonment *(Acts 24–26).* When Paul took the offering of the churches to Jerusalem, he was almost killed by his Jewish antagonists. He was rescued from certain death more than once by the Roman soldiers in Jerusalem. For his own safety the Romans took Paul to Caesarea on the Mediterranean Sea. There he stood trial before two Roman governors. Paul's Caesarea imprisonment lasted two years. When it became clear that he was not going to receive a fair trial in Caesarea, Paul exercised his rights as a Roman citizen. He demanded a trial before the emperor in Rome. Paul's years in Caesarea were AD 58–60.

Rome journey *(Acts 27–28).* Paul's journey to Rome was harrowing. The ship's captain made the terrible mistake of setting out across the open sea at the time of year when normally all shipping stopped. A hurricane drove the ship for two weeks across the water. The sailors threw the ship's cargo overboard. They lost all control of the vessel. Paul reassured the terrified passengers that there would be no loss of life if they all stayed together. Finally, the ship ran aground and broke apart. People were close enough to swim to shore or float on debris. The cold and wet passengers found themselves on the island of Malta. They remained there several months before sailing on to Italy on another vessel. Paul and his Roman guard walked the last few miles to Rome.

Great Miracles

Eight miracles are recorded during the Pauline period:
- **Prison release**
- **Smiting of Herod**
- **Smiting of a sorcerer**

- ❖ **Healing of lame man**
- ❖ **Speaking in languages**
- ❖ **Raising of Eutychus**
- ❖ **Surviving a viper's bite**
- ❖ **Healing of an official's father**

Peter was arrested by King Herod. The plan was to execute Peter after the Passover holiday. Peter was sleeping between two soldiers and had shackles on his wrists. An angel appeared in the cell. The shackles fell off, the prison doors swung open, and Peter walked out of the prison. This ***prison release*** no doubt saved Peter's life (Acts 12:5-10).

King Herod (grandson of Herod the Great) was making a speech to a large crowd in a stadium at Caesarea. To flatter the king, the people likened Herod's voice to that of a god. Because the king accepted such blasphemous flattery, the angel of the Lord ***smote Herod***. The king was eaten by worms and died. His death brought temporary relief from persecution of the church in Palestine (Acts 12:21-23).

On the island of Cyprus a Jewish sorcerer named Bar-Jesus tried to interfere with the preaching of the gospel to a Roman governor. Paul announced that God was about to ***smite the sorcerer*** with blindness for a time. Immediately mist and darkness came over him. This demonstration of God's awesome power led to the conversion of the governor (Acts 13:11).

In the city of Lystra Paul noticed in the crowd ***a lame man***. He could see that the man had the faith to be healed. Paul called out to the man and commanded him to stand up. The man was immediately healed (Acts 14:8-10).

Paul encountered twelve disciples of John the Baptist in the city of Ephesus. When these men heard the complete gospel they were baptized. Paul laid his hands on the twelve men. At that moment the Holy Spirit came upon them, and they ***spoke in unlearned languages*** and prophesied (Acts 19:6).

Pauline Period

While Paul was preaching late at night in the city of Troas, a listener fell out of a third-story window and was killed. Paul embraced the young man and then announced that he was alive (Acts 20:7-12). The *raising of Eutychus* (*ewe´-tih-khuhs*) from the dead parallels the raising of Dorcas by Peter in the Pouring Period.

While gathering sticks on the island of Malta, Paul was bitten by a ***deadly viper***. The local people thought he would die within seconds. Paul, however, showed no ill effects from the bite (Acts 28:3-4).

The governor of Malta had a *father* suffering from fever and dysentery. Paul prayed before he *healed* this man. This is the only recorded prayer before a miracle of healing in Acts. The superstitious people of the island thought Paul was a god. By praying he signaled to them that he was only a man (Acts 28:7-9).

God's Message

A large part of Christian doctrine is presented in the fifteen New Testament books written during the Pauline Period. Pagewise these letters constitute a third of the New Testament. For the purposes of this simplified overview of New Testament history we can classify the most important revelations of the Pauline Period under five heads:

- ❖ **Christ**
- ❖ **Cross**
- ❖ **Covenant**
- ❖ **Church**
- ❖ **Coming**

Christ. The Holy Spirit guided Paul in developing the doctrine of Christ especially in his letters to the Ephesians and the Philippians. Christ was the image of God (Colossians 1:15). In Christ all the fullness of deity dwelled (Colossians 2:9). When Christ came into this world, he emptied himself of heavenly glory and took upon himself the form of a servant, even becoming obedient unto death (Philippians 2:5-11). Christ is superior to the Old Testament prophets (Hebrews 1:1-3), superior to angels (Hebrews 1:4-14), superior to Moses (Hebrews 3:1-6), and superior to the Old Testament priesthood (Hebrews 5).

Cross. The doctrine of the Cross can be summed up like this: The wages of sin is death (Romans 6:23). Therefore, we deserve to die eternally for our sins. Christ died for our sins (Romans 5:8; 1 Corinthians 15:3; 1 Peter 3:18). He died as a ransom to set us free from the penalty of eternal death (Hebrews 9:15; 1 Timothy 2:6).

Covenant. Christ instituted a new covenant (Hebrews 9:15) that supersedes the old covenant established by Moses (Hebrews 8:7). Under this covenant (divine agreement) God promises to confer certain blessings upon those who put their faith in Christ as God's Son. These blessings include the forgiveness of sins, the indwelling presence of the Holy Spirit, and eternal life. The new covenant is celebrated at a symbolic meal each week at the Lord's Table (Acts 20:7; 1 Corinthians 11:25). This new covenant is superior to the old (2 Corinthians 3:6; Hebrews 7:22).

Church. The doctrine of the church is stressed especially in the letter to the Ephesians. The church is the body of Christ (Ephesians 1:23), the bride of Christ (Ephesians 5:25-27), and his kingdom on this earth (Colossians 1:12-13). Christ is the head of the church; he has all authority in it (Ephesians 1:22). The church consists of all those who have been saved from their sins (Acts 2:47) whether Jew or Gentile (Ephesians 2:14-18). Local congregations are set in order by evangelists (2 Timothy 4:5; Acts 21:8) and administered by overseers assisted by deacons (Philippians 1:1). The church has the responsibility to expel those who live lifestyles that are contrary to Christian teaching (1 Corinthians 5:13) or who teach false doctrine (Titus 3:10).

Coming. During the Pauline Period more information about the second coming of Christ was forthcoming. A great falling away from God will precede Christ's coming. The man of lawlessness will be revealed—someone who will make pretensions of deity and employ deceitful signs and wonders (2 Thessalonians 2:3-9). When Christ returns, the dead in Christ shall rise first. Then living Christians will be transformed in the twinkling of an eye into their immortal bodies. They will be caught up to meet the Lord and so shall they ever be with the Lord (1 Thessalonians 4:13-18). At the same time those who do not know God or do not obey the gospel will be punished with everlasting fire (2 Thessalonians 1:6-10). Christians will stand before the judgment seat of Christ to receive rewards for what they have done since becoming Christians (2 Corinthians 5:10).

Old Testament Anticipation

Isaiah the prophet anticipated the day when the light of the gospel was to be taken to the Gentiles. Paul cited Isaiah 49:6 in justification of his mission to the Gentiles. *"For this is what the Lord has commanded us: 'I have made you a light for the Gentiles, that you may bring salvation to the ends of the earth'"* (Acts 13:47).

Watershed Event

Nero's first five years as Roman emperor (AD 54–59) were glorious. He was guided by his wise counselor Seneca. During these years Paul executed his citizenship rights to appeal for a hearing before Caesar. He sailed to Rome in AD 60. Paul awaited trial before Nero AD 61–63.

Paul's first Roman imprisonment was more like house arrest. Paul was allowed to meet with guests. He wrote four books of the New Testament during this period: Ephesians, Colossians, Philippians and Philemon. Paul also may have written the Book of Hebrews while he was in Rome. At this point the Book of Acts ends the record of Paul's life. He was, however, released after two years when his accusers from Jerusalem never appeared to prosecute him.

With the confinement of Paul in AD 61–63 the Pauline Period of biblical history came to an end.

Summary Chart

\multicolumn{6}{c}{Period # 16 PAULINE PERIOD Acts 12–28}					
P O U R I N G	Pre-Missionary Activity Tarsus Antioch	Missionary Travels Cyprus "Turkey" Greece	Custody Period Caesarea Rome	P R I S O N
Cornelius	Acts 11:19–12:25	Acts 13–20	Acts 21–28	Paul
AD 39	AD 39–44	AD 45–58	AD 58–62	AD 63

Pauline Period

Chapter Eighteen

PERSECUTION PERIOD
The Fiery Trial

Jesus warned his followers that they would face persecution. Almost from the birthday of the church that prediction was fulfilled. At first the Christians were concentrated in the Jerusalem area. They ran afoul of the temple officials because they publicly indicted the Jewish leaders for crucifying Jesus. They also boldly declared the resurrection of Jesus from the dead, something the temple officials found particularly offensive. About four years into the history of the church the persecution in Jerusalem turned particularly ugly. Stephen was stoned to death. The Christians scattered. The temple officials commissioned agents to go to distant cities to arrest Christians and bring them back to Jerusalem for trial. The conversion of Saul of Tarsus brought an end to this phase of persecution (Acts 9).

Government officials got involved in persecuting Christians fourteen years into the history of the church (AD 44). King Herod Agrippa I (grandson of Herod the Great) arrested the Apostle James in Jerusalem and executed him. He arrested Peter with the same intention. Peter escaped certain death when an angel released him from prison. This first persecution by government ended when the king died a particularly loathsome death shortly after the execution of James (Acts 12).

Paul faced opposition from local government officials in many of the cities where he traveled. Usually the local Jewish population stirred up the city fathers against Paul.

The Emperor Nero unleashed the first imperial persecution against Christians. A second imperial persecution was launched thirteen years later by the Emperor Domitian. Bounded by horrible persecutions at the beginning and the end, no title is more appropriate for the final years of biblical history than the title Persecution Period.

The history of Christianity following Paul's first imprisonment in Rome must be reconstructed from hints given in the books of **1 & 2 Timothy, Titus, Hebrews, 1 & 2 Peter, 1, 2, 3 John, Jude,** and **Revelation**.

Duration

The Book of Acts closes with Paul in confinement in Rome. The year was AD 63. We used that event to mark the conclusion of the Pauline Period for three reasons. First, that is where Luke, author of Acts, drew the curtain on Paul's life. Second, what we know of Paul's life subsequent to Acts 28 is sketchy. Third, the years following Paul's first confinement in Rome are characterized by two great imperial persecutions. So the years following AD 63 are best viewed as a distinct period of biblical history.

The Emperor Domitian came to the throne in AD 81. Early Christian historians speak of a persecution against Christians in the reign of Domitian during which the Apostle John was exiled. A date of about AD 96 for John's exile and the writing of the Book of Revelation is probably close. John died during the reign of the Emperor Trajan, probably about AD 100. That date makes a good conclusion for biblical history. So the Persecution Period can be dated AD 63–100, about **37 years**.

Scriptural Theme

Christian tradition relates that Peter died during the persecution by Nero near the time of Paul's death. The following passage was probably penned during that persecution. It sets the tone for the Persecution Period.

Persecution Period

> *Dear friends, do not be surprised at the painful trial you are suffering, as though something strange were happening to you. But rejoice that you participate in the sufferings of Christ, so that you may be overjoyed when his glory is revealed. If you are insulted because of the name of Christ, you are blessed, for the Spirit of glory and of God rests on you. If you suffer, it should not be as a murderer or thief or any other kind of criminal, or even as a meddler. However, if you suffer as a Christian, do not be ashamed, but praise God that you bear that name* (1 Peter 4:12-16).

Key Players

In the final period of biblical history four individuals can be identified as prominent leaders in the church. Three of these were identified as key players in earlier periods of New Testament history.

- ❖ **Peter**
- ❖ **Paul**
- ❖ **John**
- ❖ **Jude**

Peter. The travels of Peter after the Jerusalem conference (Acts 15) are not recorded in detail. At some point he visited Antioch (Galatians 2:11ff) and probably Corinth (1 Corinthians 1:12). He is closely associated with Christians in five Roman provinces located in modern Turkey (1 Peter 1:1). Strong Christian tradition indicates that he made a trip to Rome. He almost certainly wrote his first letter from Rome, which he calls *Babylon* after the sinful Old Testament city (1 Peter 5:13). Shortly thereafter Peter wrote his second letter, which also is found in the New Testament.

Peter was one of the key players in the Pouring Period and the Pauline Period. His prominence continued into the early months of the Persecution Period. Peter died during the persecution by Nero.

Paul. After being released from custody in Rome, Paul resumed his missionary activity. Some of his travels during this period can be reconstructed from notes in his letters. It appears that he traveled as far as Spain preaching the gospel. During these travels Paul wrote two letters: 1 Timothy and Titus. Eventually he returned to Rome. By this time the Emperor Nero had launched an assault on Christians. Paul was arrested. While he was awaiting his execution, he wrote the letter we call 2 Timothy. This is the last letter that Paul ever wrote.

Need Help in Remembering Paul's Ministry?	
Three Journeys	**Three Jails**
"Turkey"	Caesarea
Europe	Rome
Ephesus	Rome

John. The Beloved Disciple was a major figure in the Pouring Period when he was the partner of Peter. He disappeared during the Pauline period, except for one mention. Paul regarded John as one of the *pillars of the church* (Galatians 2:9). After the destruction of Jerusalem John seems to have moved to Ephesus, which is on the western coast of modern day Turkey. After the martyrdom of Paul and Peter, John became the leading figure in the church. Of the original twelve apostles he was the last survivor.

Jude. Practically nothing is known about Jude, except that he wrote a letter—actually more of a postcard—that is part of the New Testament. This letter begins: *Jude, a servant of Jesus Christ and brother of James.* Since James was such a common name in that period, there is only one James who could be referred to in this way without further specification—*James the Lord's brother* (Galatians 1:19). So Jude must be a shortened form of Judas, one of the half-brothers of Jesus (Matthew 13:55; Mark 6:3).

Persecution Period

Persecution Period

Major Events

Only four important events transpired during the Persecution Period.

❖ Nero's persecution
❖ James's martyrdom
❖ Jerusalem's destruction
❖ John's exile

Nero's persecution. Emperor Nero's second five years (AD 60-64) were hellish. Nero became first a comic character. He had an insane appetite for popular applause; he played the lyre and sang his odes at supper; he drove his chariots in the circus; he appeared as a mimic on the stage. Gradually Nero turned into a treacherous figure: he heaped crime upon crime until he became a proverbial monster of iniquity. He murdered his wives, his teacher, his mother and brothers, not to mention many of the noblest citizens of Rome. Nero's persecution grew out of the burning of the city of Rome in AD 64. The fire lasted ten days. Ten of the fourteen districts of Rome were destroyed. Public rumor traced the burning to Nero. Nero diverted suspicion from himself by blaming the Christians.

Christian tradition places the **martyrdom of Paul** in the last year of Nero, AD 68. Tradition has it that Peter stood trial along with Paul. Both were executed. Because he was a Roman citizen, Paul was spared prolonged agony by being beheaded. Peter was sentenced to crucifixion. By his own request he was crucified upside down. He did not feel worthy to be crucified in the same position as his Master. Tradition is mixed about where the bodies of the two great apostles were buried.

The Roman historian Tacitus (*Annals* 15.44) gives a graphic description of what transpired.

> To kill rumors, Nero charged and tortured some people hated for their evil practices—the group popularly known as 'Christians'. The founder of this sect,

Christ, had been put to death by the governor of Judea, Pontius Pilate, when Tiberius was Emperor. Their deadly superstition had been suppressed temporarily, but was beginning to spring up again—not now just in Judea but even in Rome itself where all kinds of sordid and shameful activities are attracted and catch on. First, those who confessed to being Christians were arrested. Then, on information obtained from them, hundreds were convicted, more for their anti-social beliefs than for fire-raising. In their deaths they were made a mockery. They were covered in the skins of wild animals, torn to death by dogs, crucified or set on fire—so that when darkness fell they burned like torches in the night. Nero opened up his own gardens for this spectacle and gave a show in the arena, where he mixed with the crowd, or stood dressed as a charioteer on a chariot. As a result, although they were guilty of being Christians and deserved death, people began to feel sorry for them. For they realized that they were being massacred not for the public good but to satisfy one man's mania.

There is some dispute as to the extent of Nero's persecution. Roman historians are silent about the spread of this persecution to the provinces. Later Christian writers, however, affirm that Christians throughout the Roman world were persecuted during Nero's reign. Possible biblical allusions to this persecution are found in Hebrews 10:32-34; 1 Peter 2:12, 19-20; 3:14-18; 4:12-19.

Nero committed suicide at the age of 32. With his death the family of the great Julius Caesar perished. There was anarchy in the Roman Empire after Nero's Death. The throne became the prize for the strongest claimant. Historian Philip Schaff wrote: "There is scarcely another period in history so full of vice, corruption, and disaster as the six years between the Neronian persecution and the destruction of Jerusalem" (Schaff, 1.391). Here are just a few of Rome's troubles: four princes (Galba, Otho, Vitellius, Domitian) were killed by the sword. Three civil wars and several foreign wars were being conducted simultaneously. According to

Persecution Period

the Roman historian Tacitus, at the same time there were unprecedented natural disasters: fires, earthquakes and volcanic eruptions destroying whole cities (Tacitus, *History*, 1.2). Christians suffered, not only from direct persecution but from all the upheavals going on throughout the empire.

James's martyrdom. James (Jesus' brother) died a martyr's death in Jerusalem. One account says he was stoned; another says he was thrown from the highest point of the temple. Perhaps both accounts are true. James the Lord's brother died about AD 66.

Jerusalem's destruction. Both Daniel (9:26-27; ch. 12) and Jesus (Matthew 24:1-34; Luke 19:43-44) prophesied the destruction of Jerusalem by the Romans. Jesus told his disciples to flee Jerusalem when they saw *the abomination of desolation* spoken of by Daniel standing in the holy place (Matthew 24:15). Luke 21:20 makes clear that this mysterious terminology refers to an army. The Roman army carried standards that were considered idols by the Jews, hence *abomination. Desolation* describes what the Roman army did to the temple and the city of Jerusalem.

The Christians did exactly what their Master told them to do when they saw a Roman army approach Jerusalem, but then suddenly withdraw. The Christians evacuated. According to the historian Eusebius, the Christians took refuge across the Jordan River in a vacated city called Pella (*Ecclesiastical History*, 3.5).

Jerusalem suffered mightily during the Roman siege. A three-way civil war raged within the city while the Romans were attacking from without. The Romans crucified hundreds of prisoners every day within sight of the city. Famine raged. Thousands died daily inside the city. Zealots gained control. They launched a reign of terror against any who might be inclined to surrender to the Romans. Reports of comets, meteors, and all sorts of fearful omens were interpreted as signs of the coming Messiah.

Finally the Romans broke through the defenses. They burned and razed Jerusalem. Only three towers were left standing as a testimony to the strength of the city that defied the Romans for four years. The Jewish historian Josephus gives the figure of those slain as 1,100,000. Another 11,000 perished of starvation shortly after the close of the siege. Some 97,000 were taken as slaves or to die in the gladiatorial shows.

The fall of Jerusalem in AD 70 was important to Christians for two reasons. First, it fulfilled predictions made by Jesus forty years earlier. Thus Jesus was shown to be a true prophet. Second, the destruction of the temple led to a separation of Judaism and Christianity that was complete and permanent.

John's exile. The last recorded event of New Testament history is the exile of the Apostle John to the island of Patmos (Revelation 1:9). Patmos (*pat´-muhs*) was a small, rocky, barren island about ten miles long and six miles wide. John was on Patmos when he received the visions that he recorded in the Book of Revelation. Pliny, the Roman writer, mentions Patmos as a place to which undesirable people were banished. Emperors used banishment as a means to rid themselves of influential troublemakers without having to make martyrs of them.

Great Miracles

No great miracles are recorded in Scripture during the Persecution Period. John symbolizes the power of prayer by mention of miracles. He paints the picture of two witnesses (symbolizing God's church) being slain, then rising from the dead (Revelation 11:11-12). This probably symbolizes a great final revival of God's church just prior to the end of the age.

God's Message

Twelve books of the New Testament were written during this period. As might be expected, the major issue during the Persecution Period was how Christians should respond to persecution. Entire books like 1 Peter, Hebrews, and Revelation were written to encourage Christians in a situation of persecution (1 Peter 3:13-18; 4:12-19; 5:6-14; Hebrews 10:32-39; 12:3; Revelation 2–3). The

New Testament teaching is that persecution should be faced with patience, endurance, and steadfastness (Romans 12:12; 1 Thessalonians 2:14-16; James 5:7-11); prayer (Matthew 5:44; Romans 12:14; 1 Corinthians 4:12); and thanksgiving (2 Thessalonians 1:4). Such difficulties served the purpose of testing (Mark 4:17) and strengthening of faith (1 Thessalonians 3:2-3). In suffering, Christians experience the grace of God (Romans 8:35; 2 Corinthians 4:9, 12:10), and blessing (Matthew 5:10-12; 1 Peter 3:14; 4:12-14). Persecution provided a Christian with an opportunity to be a living and visible testimony to the crucified and risen Christ (2 Corinthians 4:7-12).

Space only permits a few examples of the interesting things God revealed to his people in the inspired literature of the Persecution Period. This revelation focuses on the following:

- ❖ **Distant past**
- ❖ **Recent past**
- ❖ **Present**
- ❖ **Near future**
- ❖ **Distant future**

Distant past. Two passages written during the Persecution Period shed light on the origin of Satan (2 Peter 2:4; Jude 1:6). At some point, even before the creation of the world, heavenly angels sinned in some manner against God. Jude says they *"did not keep their positions of authority but abandoned their own home"* (1:6). These rebellious angels had a leader. His name is Satan or the devil. The rebellious angels are kept in darkness. They are bound with everlasting chains for final judgment.

Recent past. In the recent past (from the standpoint of the New Testament writers) Christ had done his work on the Cross. The Book of Revelation, using highly symbolic language, describes the efforts of Satan (depicted as a red dragon) to destroy Christ at birth. When Christ ascended to heaven, there was war in heaven (the spiritual realm). Michael the archangel and his angels fought against the dragon and his angels. In symbolic language John is depicting how Satan tried his best to prevent the enthronement of Christ in heaven; but he failed. The dragon was thrown down to earth where he tried his best to destroy the woman who gave birth to Christ. She symbolizes God's people (Revelation 12).

The present. The enthroned Christ sent seven letters to Christian congregations (Revelation 2-3). In these letters he reveals the present conditions—good and bad—in each church. Congregations are urged to repent. Individuals are encouraged to be faithful. Jude describes at length the false teachers that had gone forth into the church. In his three epistles John also battles these false teachers who denied that Christ had a flesh and blood body. John calls them antichrists (1 John 2:18-22).

Near future. There is much discussion among Christian teachers about how much of the symbolism of the Revelation applies to the near future (from John's standpoint) and how much to the "end times." Most would acknowledge, however, that John reveals the near future of the seven churches to which Christ sent letters in Revelation 2-3. Peter warns of the rise of scoffers who mock the idea of a second coming of Christ (2 Peter 3).

Distant future. Peter speaks of the fiery end of the world and the subsequent new heavens and earth (2 Peter 3:12). Revelation depicts Satan released at the end of the thousand (symbolic) years of Christ's reign. He goes forth to deceive the nations with paganism as he did before the gospel came into the world (Revelation 20). John depicts in symbols the beauties of the heavenly Jerusalem (Revelation 21-22).

Old Testament Anticipation

Persecuted Christians need to be reminded that Christ is enthroned in heaven. He rules with an iron scepter (Revelation 2:27; 12:5). This iron-scepter rule of Christ was anticipated by the prophet David: *"You will rule them with an iron scepter; you will dash them to pieces like pottery"* (Psalms 2:9).

Persecution Period

Persecution Period

Watershed Event

The popular Emperor Titus died at the untimely age of forty-two, after only two years+ as emperor. He was succeeded by his thirty-year-old brother Domitian. He came to the throne a despised younger brother, embittered by his elders' contempt.

Domitian ruthlessly removed all who opposed him. The anti-Christian policy of Nero, sporadically pursued under emperors Vespasian and Titus, was vigorously implemented. Domitian proclaimed himself *lord and god*. In Rome, but especially in the provinces, temples were built to Domitian. Roman officials were suspicious of the loyalties of Christians because they refused to offer incense to the statue of the emperor. It was during this time that the Apostle John was exiled to the island of Patmos where he received the visions later recorded in the Book of Revelation. This occurred about the year AD 96. John died about the year AD 100. This marks the end of the Persecution Period of biblical history.

Summary Chart

	Period # 17 PERSECUTION PERIOD 1 & 2 Timothy, Titus, Hebrews, 1 & 2 Peter, 1–3 John, Jude, Revelation						
CONFINED	Deaths of Peter & Paul c. AD 68	Destruction of Jerusalem AD 70			Patmos Exile AD 96		DIED
Paul	Emperor Nero	Emperor Vespasian	Emperor Titus	Emperor Domitian		Emperor Trajan	John
AD 63	54–68	69–79	79–81	81–96		98–117	AD 100

A FINAL WORD

Our journey on the path of biblical history is now over. We have traveled from the beautiful Paradise of Genesis to the ugly island of Patmos. Our journey has surveyed more than 2,200 years of God's dealings with mankind. We have climbed great mountains of divine revelation and descended into deep valleys of spiritual darkness. Along our path we have met the powerful and the pathetic, the godly and the godless, those woefully weak in faith and those faith giants that challenge our level of commitment today. We have witnessed stupendous miracles, and endured depressing times when it seemed that God had turned his back on his people.

In our journey we have traveled through seventeen time zones. One was as short as ten years; others lasted three and even four centuries. Two of the time zones were of unknown duration. From the vantage point of our completed journey we are in a position to make some general observations about biblical history. Please take a moment to reflect on these tie-it-all-together questions.

- ❖ **What have I learned about God?**
- ❖ **The most memorable character in each Testament?**
- ❖ **What have I learned about sin?**
- ❖ **What have I learned about salvation?**
- ❖ **The most important miracle in each Testament?**

ABBREVIATIONS

KJV .... King James Version
NASB .... New American Standard Bible
NIV .... New International Version

OTHER BOOKS BY THE AUTHOR

Available from College Press, Joplin, Mo. www.collegepress.com
  The Pentateuch, 1993, 534 pp.
  The Books of History, 1995, 747 pp.
  The Wisdom Literature and Psalms, 1996, 873 pp.
  The Major Prophets, 1992, 637 pp.
  The Minor Prophets, 1994, 653 pp.
  1 & 2 Samuel in "The College Press NIV Commentary," 2000. 541 pp.
  Old Testament Books Made Simple, 2009, 237 pp.
  New Testament Books Made Simple, 2009, 177 pp.

Also by this author:
  What the Bible Says about the Promised Messiah 1991, 522 pp.
  Biblical Protology, 2007, 530 pp.
  Postexilic Prophets, 2007, 268 pp.
  Daniel: a Christian Interpretation, 2008, 416 pp.
  Ezekiel: a Christian Interpretation, 2008, 468 pp.
  Jeremiah: a Christian Interpretation, 2008, 540 pp.

For articles and commentaries and other materials, check the author's web site: bibleprofessor.com

www.ingramcontent.com/pod-product-compliance
Lightning Source LLC
Chambersburg PA
CBHW070549050426
42450CB00011B/2787